(65 - 13706)

JUL 12 '68

THE
MONROE DOCTRINE

Its Modern Significance

Borzoi Books ON LATIN AMERICA

General Editor

LEWIS HANKE

COLUMBIA UNIVERSITY

THE
MONROE
DOCTRINE

Its Modern Significance

❖❖❖❖❖❖❖❖❖

EDITED WITH AN INTRODUCTION BY

Donald Marquand Dozer

UNIVERSITY OF CALIFORNIA,
SANTA BARBARA

19  65

NEW YORK: *Alfred · A · Knopf*

NOTE: Several selections in this book, as indicated in the source footnotes, have not heretofore appeared in English translation. These have been translated by Donald Marquand Dozer.

L. C. catalog card number: 65–13706

THIS IS A BORZOI BOOK,

PUBLISHED BY ALFRED A. KNOPF, INC.

SECOND PRINTING, AUGUST 1967

DEDICATED TO

James Phinney Baxter III

IN GRATITUDE

"I only know two things about the Monroe Doctrine: one is that no American I have met knows what it is; the other is that no American I have met will consent to its being tampered with. . . . I conclude that the Monroe Doctrine is not a doctrine but a dogma, . . . not one dogma but two, to wit: the dogma of the infallibility of the American President and the dogma of the immaculate conception of American foreign policy."

Salvador de Madariaga,
*Latin America between the Eagle
and the Bear,* NEW YORK, 1962, p. 74.

Foreword

The theme of this book is the Monroe Doctrine viewed as an essential element in United States foreign policy and inter-American relations in the twentieth century. The Introduction broadly traces the origin and historical evolution of the Doctrine from 1823 to the present, analyzes the various constructions which have been placed upon it, and introduces the selections which follow. These include review articles, outstanding addresses, editorials, and official policy statements dealing with this multifaceted Doctrine. The selections, arranged in approximate chronological order, have been chosen because they illustrate effectively, as only original documents can do, the major interpretations of the Doctrine and the principal varieties of reactions to it since 1898. This volume is not limited to material from the United States or even the Western Hemisphere, though for obvious reasons selections from this hemisphere predominate. But the extension of United States interests into other continents—Europe, Asia, and Africa—during and since World War I has affected the Monroe Doctrine in crucial ways and given it a measure of international significance extending beyond the Western Hemisphere. The selections which follow reflect the present world-wide interests of the United States.

Grateful acknowledgement is made to the original authors and publishers of these selections for their consent to republish them here, and whenever necessary specific acknowledgement is made with each selection. The editor of this Borzoi series, Professor Lewis Hanke of Columbia University, has been unfailingly helpful with sound suggestions and valuable insights. In addition, I wish to recognize with deep appreciation the help of the following staff members of the library of the University of California, Santa Barbara: Mrs. Dorothy Annable, Mrs. Vivian Karschner, Mrs. Cordelia English, and Mr. Ronald Silvera. And for assistance far over and beyond the call of duty I am especially indebted to Mr. Lewis Tambs, now assistant professor of history at Creighton University, Omaha, Nebraska.

Donald Marquand Dozer

Santa Barbara, California

Contents

Chronological Highlights
of the Monroe Doctrine

1823, December 2. Monroe Doctrine first promulgated by President James Monroe in annual message to Congress.

1845, December 2. Reasserted by President James K. Polk in annual message to Congress.

1848, April 29. Reaffirmed by President Polk in special message to Congress relating to Yucatan.

1867, February. Vindicated by withdrawal of troops of Napoleon III from Mexico.

1895, July 20. Applied by Secretary of State Richard Olney in Great Britain-Venezuela boundary dispute.

1895, December 17. Made the subject of special message to Congress by President Grover Cleveland in Great Britain-Venezuela boundary dispute.

1902, December 29. Economic corollary to Monroe Doctrine proposed by Dr. Luis M. Drago, Argentine Minister of Foreign Affairs, declaring "that the public debt cannot occasion armed intervention nor the actual occupation of the territory of American nations by a European power."

1904, December 6. Corollary to Monroe Doctrine announced by President Theodore Roosevelt in annual message to Congress.

1912, July 31. Magdalena Bay resolution introduced into Senate and subsequently passed.

1919, June 28. Monroe Doctrine defined as a "regional understanding" in Covenant of League of Nations.

1928, December 17. J. Reuben Clark, *Memorandum on the Monroe Doctrine* published and in 1930 distributed.

1938, December 9–24. Principle of continental solidarity against threats from abroad recognized at Eighth Inter-American Conference, Lima, Peru.

1939, September 23–October 3. Belligerent acts by participants in World War II excluded from Western Hemisphere at First Meeting of Ministers of Foreign Affairs, Panama.

1940, June 17. No-transfer principle affirmed by United States in notes to European governments.

1940, July 21–30. No-transfer principle approved and measures implementing it adopted at Second Meeting of Ministers of Foreign Affairs, Havana, Cuba.

1942, January 15–28. Inter-American measures of cooperative resistance to foreign intervention adopted at Third Meeting of Ministers of Foreign Affairs, Rio de Janeiro, Brazil.

1945, February 21–March 8. Territorial integrity and political independence of American states guaranteed in declaration of Inter-American Conference on Problems of War and Peace, Mexico City.

1947, August 15–September 2. Preceding guaranty embodied in Inter-American Treaty of Reciprocal Assistance (Pact of Rio de Janeiro), signed at Inter-American Conference for the Maintenance of Continental Peace and Security, Quitandinha, Brazil.

1954, March 1–28. Declaration of American opposition to the international Communist movement at the Tenth Inter-American Conference.

1960, July 14. Monroe Doctrine reaffirmed by State Department.

1962, October 22. "Retaliatory response" threatened by President John F. Kennedy against nuclear attack from Cuba.

THE
MONROE DOCTRINE
Its Modern Significance

Introduction

The Monroe Doctrine underlies and explains a considerable part of the history of United States foreign policy, particularly the history of inter-American relations. The very word *Monroeism* is sometimes used to comprehend everything that deals with the relations between the United States and Latin America.[1] And yet, one Latin-American commentator has somewhat cynically observed, "The Monroe Doctrine is neither a doctrine nor is it Monroe's. It is not a doctrine because doctrines are fixed, invariable, they resolve problems of similar nature in the same way, but the Monroe Doctrine resolves them according to the caprice and convenience of its interpreters; and it is not Monroe's because that President did no more than sign the message which contained it, and its true authors were Canning, Jefferson, Madison, and especially Adams."[2] And a Venezuelan writer going still further insists that the Monroe Doctrine in reality "cannot be interpreted . . . either as to its origins, as to the course of historical events which determined its formulation, as to the meaning of its careful and deliberate language, or as to its spirit."[3]

The Doctrine which has come to bear the name of President James Monroe was promulgated by him in his annual message to Congress on December 2, 1823. Both its meaning and its precise status as a tenet of foreign policy have been subjects of perennial controversy. The Doctrine was first set forth as a unilateral pronouncement of policy for the United States in dealing with a specific problem, namely, the incursion or threatened incursion of European powers into

[1] See, e.g., Juan A. Ortega y Medina, "Monroísmo Arqueológico," *Cuadernos Americanos,* Nos. 5–6, 1953, pp. 168–189.

[2] Félix Pérez Porta, "La Doctrina de Monroe," *Cuba Contemporánea,* Havana, XXVIII (January 1922), 45.

[3] Jacinto López in *Revista Social,* New York, quoted in Isidro Fabela, *Las Doctrinas Monroe y Drago* (Mexico: Universidad Nacional Autónoma de Mexico, 1957), p. 72.

the Western Hemisphere. It is a doctrine of the defense of the United States, or, as Secretary of State Lewis Cass later called it, the American doctrine of self-preservation. As originally promulgated it responded to a concept of national interest which the United States had taken over from the European powers. When Monroe set forth the principles which have since been associated with his name as a policy of the United States, he based them upon "our peace and safety."

In that message he asserted first, "as a principle in which the rights and interests of the United States are involved, that the American continents, by the free and independent condition which they have assumed and maintained, are henceforth not to be considered as subjects for future colonization by any European powers." This principle was intended to thwart the territorial pretensions of the Russian Czar Alexander I along the northwest coast of the North American continent. A specific warning to this effect had already been pointedly communicated by Secretary of State John Quincy Adams to the Czar's government, and in Monroe's message it was broadened into a general principle.

This principle assumed that all the territory in the American continents had already been effectively colonized, which was far from true, for in 1823 large areas in the American hemisphere were void of people, and national boundary lines were not clearly defined. But, as the Mexican writer Antonio Gómez Robledo has ingeniously argued, Monroe's warning against European colonization in the New World was simply a political affirmation of the international law principle of *uti possidetis,* that is, each nation should be recognized as possessing the territory to which it had legal claim and was entitled to have its territorial integrity respected by other nations. In this sense the territory of the American hemisphere was not open to colonization. Although boundary lines between the new nations were still, in many cases, subjects of controversy, no part of the American continents could be considered as *res nullius,* that is, belonging to no one. Monroe, it should be noted, in warning European powers against further colonization in the American continents, did not specifically preclude the American nations, including the United States, from the privilege of engaging in such colonization.

In Monroe's message, the President followed his warning

against future colonization in the American continents by any European powers with a warning to "the allied powers" of Europe, namely the members of the Quadruple Alliance—France, Austria, Russia, and Prussia—that "we should consider any attempt on their part to extend their system to any portion of this hemisphere as dangerous to our peace and safety. With the existing colonies or dependencies of any European power," Monroe continued, "we have not interfered and shall not interfere. But with the governments who have declared their independence and maintained it, and whose independence we have, on great consideration and on just principles, acknowledged, we could not view any interposition for the purpose of oppressing them, or controlling in any other manner their destiny, by any European power in any other light than as the manifestation of an unfriendly disposition toward the United States."

The "system" of the allied powers which if extended to any portion of this hemisphere would, as Monroe proclaimed, be "dangerous to our peace and safety" was the system of monarchical legitimacy which had been used to restore displaced sovereigns to European thrones after the Napoleonic wars and which, it was feared, would once more be imposed upon Spain's former kingdoms in America by the combined military efforts of the Quadruple Alliance powers. The possibility of such action by the European coalition has been variously estimated, but it seems clear that it was not so serious as Monroe and Adams believed it to be. Though the armies of Spain were still trying to suppress the "rebel" movements in America, their repeated defeats obviously were rendering Spain's cause hopeless.

Britain had already pulled away from the European coalition, was profitably exploiting the commercial potentialities of the new nations in the Americas, and had no desire to see them restored to the mercantilist embrace of Spain. In August 1823 when French assistance to Spain in the reconquest of the revolting American states seemed imminent, the British Foreign Minister, George Canning, broached to Richard Rush, the United States Minister in London, a proposal for a joint declaration by the two governments against such reconquest, but he soon afterward received assurances from the French Ambassador in London, the Prince de Polignac—assurances which he did not trouble to communicate to Washington—that France "abjured, in any case, any design of acting against the colonies by force of arms." Meanwhile Emperor Francis I of Austria, who was the father-in-law of Dom Pedro I, the new sovereign of independent Brazil, was throwing his weight against European intervention in the Americas.

Under these circumstances the United States might have been expected to make common cause with Britain in order to preserve the independence of the new American nations and to capture Britain's burgeoning trade for the United States. Indeed, former Presidents James Madison and Thomas Jefferson whom Monroe consulted counseled this course of action. But Secretary Adams persuaded both Monroe and the Cabinet of the unwisdom of a joint declaration with Britain, arguing that "it would be more candid, as well as more dignified, to avow our principles explicitly to Russia and France than to come in as a cock-boat in the wake of the British man-of-war." Besides, since Canning had stipulated that England herself "aimed at the possession of no portion of the colonies for herself," Adams did not wish to limit the United States with a similar self-denying pledge and thus preclude from it the possibility at some future time of annexing Cuba or other Latin-American territory.

The Monroe Doctrine, therefore, in its original statement, lacked all connotation of an alliance. It was issued without the concurrence of England or of any other nation. No consultation was held with any of the new states in the Americas while it was being drawn up, and after it was announced no effort was made to obtain their cooperation in enforcing it. For well over a century the United States resisted all temptation to associate itself with other nations in upholding the principles of the Doctrine. This nation and this nation alone reserved the right both to interpret it and to implement it as suited its own interests.

Both the warnings to Europe contained in Monroe's declaration and the unilateral character of that declaration responded to the doctrine of the two spheres—a doctrine which perhaps had its origin in the Treaty of Tordesillas in 1494 and which had long been an accepted tenet of the creed of all Americans. Monroe's pronouncement represented, in the words of José Ortega y Gasset, a significant move toward "transferring the center of the universe from

Europe to America." Monroe gave novel expression to the European conception of balance of power; he applied it not as between nations but as between continents. The principles of the Doctrine rested on the conviction of a fundamental dissimilarity between the Old World doctrines of repression and the New World doctrines of liberty. The Western Hemisphere had established values and interests distinct from those of Europe which it must safeguard from subversion by alien, that is, by European forces.

In the struggle of Monroe's countrymen for independence from England, they had strengthened their Americanist point of view. They reaffirmed it in their policy of neutrality toward the wars of the French Revolution. And now Monroe gave it formal expression.

This "Western Hemisphere idea," to use Professor Arthur Whitaker's felicitous phrase, underlay Monroe's third principle pledging the United States to continued abstention from intervention in the internal affairs of the European nations. "Our policy in regard to Europe," Monroe declared, "which was adopted at an early stage of the wars which have so long agitated that quarter of the globe, nevertheless remains the same, which is not to interfere in the internal concerns of any of its powers." The third principle, thus stated, gave the Doctrine a reciprocal character. It seemed to make European nonintervention in American affairs dependent upon American nonintervention in European affairs and so gave new sanction to the concept of hemispheric isolationism. Of the three cardinal principles of the Doctrine the last alone implied self-restraint on the part of the United States, but it implied self-restraint only in relation to Europe. The Monroe Doctrine was primarily a policy pronouncement of the United States *vis-à-vis* Europe.

And yet the warnings to Europe contained in it were necessarily negative in character. As Secretary of State Richard Olney later explained, it "was silent as to the part Europe might be permitted to play in America." And, further, it did not intimate any course of conduct to be pursued in case European nations interposed their control in the Western Hemisphere. It left the United States discretion to act at all times as its opinion of its duty and interest might require. It put the United States in a posture of war without committing it to war.

The Monroe Doctrine, in its original formulation, affirmed the sovereignty of the American nations which had declared their independence and required that other nations should respect the sovereignty of those nations which had broken their colonial ties. But it had nothing to do with purely inter-American relations, and only by implication did it create a special relationship between the United States and Latin America. But as it, in fact, acknowledged such a relationship among the American nations long implicit in the doctrine of the two spheres, the Doctrine as a unilateral pronouncement of the United States contained the germs of a multilateral policy or Pan-Americanism. In it might later be found the ingredients of an American system which could perhaps be stirred together to form a Pan-American organization, but the Doctrine itself did not bind the United States to any course of action nor did it suggest any self-denial by it in relation to Latin America.[4]

The conviction in the minds of Americans of the importance of maintaining their political and ideological detachment from Europe and even their superiority over Europeans in certain respects was shared also by Latin Americans. It had been confirmed for them in their struggle for independence from their European mother countries, France, Spain, and Portugal, and was made the basis of policy by Simón Bolívar and other leaders of the independence movement in Latin America. Their acceptance of the Western Hemisphere idea which underlay Monroe's brave pronouncements has inspired some Latin-American publicists to trace the genesis of the Monroe Doctrine to the Chilean patriot Juan Egaña, the Colombian Manuel Torres, the Uruguayan José Gervasio Artigas, the Argentines Mariano Moreno and José de San Martín, even Simón Bolívar himself, and other Latin-American leaders of the struggle for continental independence. Monroe, according to a present-day Spanish scholar, Camilo Barcía Trelles, far from initiating a historic policy affirmed an old tradition common to both Anglo-America and Latin America; he merely uni-

---

[4] The influence of the "doctrine of the two spheres" on the formulation of the Monroe Doctrine has been traced, with examples, in J. Reuben Clark, *Memorandum on the Monroe Doctrine* (Washington: Government Printing Office, 1930) and Arthur P. Whitaker, *The Western Hemisphere Idea* (Ithaca, N.Y.: Cornell University Press, 1954).

lateralized it.[5] Because the Doctrine rested on the traditional bases of American policy and adumbrated a future course of action similarly based, it probably would have appeared even if neither Monroe nor Adams had lived. Indeed, it perhaps needed not to be formulated at all in order to be understood as a basis of foreign policy for the United States as well as other nations of the Americas.

The Monroe Doctrine stated a policy which the United States announced its intention of following and of imposing upon Europe with respect to the American nations. It did not set forth new principles of international law nor could the United States unilaterally do so. The Doctrine was, writes the Mexican scholar Isidro Fabela, "a political opinion, the public expression of a desire which does not imply a doctrine; for the North American people it is a counsel, for the Latin Americans a protection not asked for and not even based on consultation with them, and for the Europeans a republican ukase with the characteristics, rather, of an international impertinence, as Bismarck called it."[6]

From the time the Doctrine was first enunciated the other nations of the Americas tried to associate themselves with it and to make it a principle of inter-American law. They were convinced both by Monroe's declaration and by other factors that their interests coincided with those of the United States. Bolívar urged the Peruvian delegates to the Panama Congress in 1826 to get the Congress to publish such "an energetic and efficient declaration" against European colonization in America and European intervention in American affairs as had been made by President Monroe.[7] But not until the Lima Conference in 1847 did the Spanish-American nations adopt resolutions to this effect. Brazil, on the other hand, recognized the new doctrine from the beginning and even sought to conclude an offensive and defensive alliance with the United States on the basis of Monroe's principles—an alliance which the other states of

---

[5] Camilo Barcía Trelles, *Doctrina de Monroe y Cooperación Internacional* (Madrid: Companía Ibero-Americana de Publicaciones, S.A., Editorial Mundo Latino, 1931). See also Antonio Gómez Robledo, "Epopeya del Monroísmo," *Jus: Revista de Derecho y Ciencias Sociales*, Mexico, D. F., III (November 1939), 365–408.

[6] Isidro Fabela, *Las Doctrinas Monroe y Drago*, p. 83.

[7] W. S. Robertson, "South America and the Monroe Doctrine, 1824–1828," *Political Science Quarterly*, XXX (March 1915), 86.

South America should be invited to join. But overtures from both Brazil and Gran Colombia to convert the Monroe Doctrine into a cooperative defensive alliance of American states guaranteeing the security of the hemisphere were rebuffed by the United States. Latin Americans soon discovered that the United States intended to maintain with them only a platonic relationship. They were explicitly informed that each American nation must defend itself through its own efforts and that the United States would not apply the Doctrine unless its own interests were compromised.

This unilateral interpretation of the Monroe Doctrine constituted both a strength and a weakness, and the failure of the United States to implement the Doctrine proved disillusioning to Latin Americans. "Presidents, Secretaries of State, and Congresses after Monroe," wrote Isidro Fabela in 1957, "have interpreted his Doctrine in many different ways; some forgot it, another repudiated it, another extended it, and all together have disfigured his original concept to the advantage of the United States and to the prejudice of the peoples whom Mr. Monroe wished or said he wished to protect."[8] President Monroe himself, according to assurances which he gave to the first Argentine Minister to the United States, believed that "his declaration constituted an unequivocal promise to protect South America."[9] But Monroe's "promise," as President Guadalupe Victoria of Mexico reported regretfully to his Congress in May 1826, was not sustained by the government in Washington.[1] The United States did not invoke the Doctrine in 1833 when Britain annexed the Falkland Islands claimed by Argentina, nor when France engaged in 1838 in the so-called Pastry Cook's War with Mexico, nor in the years 1838–1840 when France blockaded the Río de la Plata.

President James K. Polk reaffirmed the Monroe Doctrine in his annual message to Congress on December 2, 1845, in

---

[8] Isidro Fabela, *Las Doctrinas Monroe y Drago*, p. 64.

[9] Thomas B. Davis, Jr., "Carlos de Alvear and James Monroe: New Light on the Origin of the Monroe Doctrine," *Hispanic-American Historical Review*, XXIII (November 1943), 637.

[1] British and Foreign State Papers, XIII, 1082, quoted in William R. Manning, "Statements, Interpretations, and Applications of the Monroe Doctrine and of More or Less Allied Doctrines, from 1823 to 1845," *Proceedings of the American Society of International Law*, Eighth Annual Meeting, Washington, D.C., April 22–25, 1914, p. 52.

which he added the so-called Polk Corollary prohibiting even the voluntary transfer of territory by an American state to any European power. In reviving the Doctrine he also broadened it, making it a specific warning against European diplomatic intrigue to maintain a balance of power in America. And he affirmed it as applying with special force to the North American continent rather than the entire hemisphere. Probably for this reason his administration did not cite the Doctrine when both France and England carried on naval and military actions in 1845–1849 against the Argentine government headed by General Manuel de Rosas, nor did his successors appeal to it in 1852–1859 in the controversy over the Islas de Bahía between Britain and Honduras and in the further extension of British control in Central America in the same decade. Although the failure of the attempt by Napoleon III to subvert the government of Mexico is sometimes credited to the Monroe Doctrine, Secretary of State William H. Seward did not once mention it by name in any official exchanges. Nor was it invoked when Spain occupied the Dominican Republic in 1861 and engaged Peru, Ecuador, and Chile in war in 1864–1866 nor when Sweden transferred her Caribbean island St. Bartholomew to France in 1878. John C. Calhoun, Polk himself on one occasion, and later Abraham Lincoln insisted that Monroe had not intended to establish a general principle but that his declarations were provoked only by a specific situation which soon ceased to exist. "These declarations," said Lincoln, "referred only to the history of that day."

By a curious logic the belief gained currency that the Doctrine remained alive only because it was supported by the British navy! Canning had emphatically repudiated the non-colonization principle of the Monroe Doctrine when he first learned of it, but he soon claimed credit for the Doctrine with the boast, "I called a New World into existence to redress the balance of the Old."

No nation violated the Doctrine more frequently than Britain throughout the nineteenth century. It was alleged that in negotiating the Clayton-Bulwer Treaty with the United States in 1850 Great Britain impliedly accepted the non-colonization principle of the Doctrine, but this supposition was belied by England's later action in the dispute with Venezuela over British Guiana involving the Monroe Doctrine in which Lord Salisbury explicitly rejected "any acceptance of it on the part of Her Majesty's Government."[2]

The Monroe Doctrine gradually came to be considered in Latin America, as well as in the United States, as embodying a policy—sometimes the whole policy—of the United States toward Latin America. For this reason, though no direct relationship could be demonstrated between the Doctrine and the territorial conquests of the United States at the expense of Mexico in 1846–1848 nor the filibustering expeditions from the United States to Nicaragua and Cuba in the 1850's, the Doctrine was viewed with apprehension by Latin Americans as a threat to their liberties. Sometimes, as even its severest critics in Latin America acknowledged, it worked beneficently for them as when, for example in 1865–1867 and in 1895, it protected them against subversion of their nationality and threats to their territorial integrity by European nations. In 1893, the Brazilian author Eduardo Prado published A Illusão Americana, a bitter indictment of the United States for its repeated failures to enforce the Monroe Doctrine, but the indictment was immediately suppressed by the Brazilian government.[3]

Under these circumstances, the Monroe Doctrine appeared in 1865 to the Argentine Minister to the United States, Domingo Faustino Sarmiento, "rather like a dark cloud than a bright light." A "Monroe Doctrine in practice" that would be "really worthy of a free people," Sarmiento declared, would inspire the United States to help the South American countries learn political responsibility and would help educate them in the same manner in which it was helping its own territories prepare for statehood—an interesting prefiguration of some of its subsequent efforts in that area.[4] But even as a defense against Europe, the Doctrine,

[2] Dexter Perkins, A History of the Monroe Doctrine (Boston: Little, Brown and Company, 1955), p. 97; and R. A. Humphreys, The Diplomatic History of British Honduras, 1638–1901 (London and New York, 1961).

[3] Eduardo Prado, A Illusão Americana, new edition with a preface by Augusto Frederico Schmidt (Rio de Janeiro: Civilização Brasileira, S.A., 1933).

[4] Address to the Rhode Island Historical Society, December 27, 1865, reprinted in Luis M. Drago, La República Argentina y el Caso de Venezuela (Buenos Aires, 1903), pp. 304–312. See also Nancy Brandt, "Don Yo in America: Domingo Faustino Sarmiento's Second Visit to the United States," The Americas, XIX (July 1962), 31.

it seemed, was being rendered obsolete by the breakdown of physical barriers between the New World and the Old. "The three Atlantic cables," Juan Bautista Alberdi wrote in 1870, "have destroyed and buried the Monroe Doctrine without the least formality."[5]

Sarmiento conceived of Monroe's pronouncement as a doctrine of cooperation among the nations of the hemisphere and not as a doctrine of United States hegemony or imperialism. It was in the former sense that it was used in the 1880's to justify the new Pan-American movement. Secretary of State Frederick T. Frelinghuysen spoke in 1884 of "the desirability of knitting closely our relations with the states of this continent . . . in the spirit of the Monroe Doctrine, which, in excluding foreign political interference, recognizes the common interest of the states of North and South America."[6] "In the spirit of the Monroe Doctrine," the new Pan-Americanism espoused by the United States represented in part a maneuver to protect both its trade and its strategic interests from European competition in Latin America. It was still grounded on the old conception of rivalry between the New World and Europe.

Long before the Monroe Doctrine was dramatically revived by President Grover Cleveland in 1895, it had come to be widely accepted, at least in the United States, as a national policy to be defended at almost all costs. Cleveland's appeal to the Doctrine, which brought his nation to the brink of war with England over a boundary dispute between Venezuela and British Guiana, confirmed its status as a national policy. During that dispute Secretary of State Olney defined the Monroe Doctrine to the British Prime Minister, Lord Salisbury, as follows:

> It does not establish any general protectorate by the United States over other American states. It does not relieve any American state from its obligations as fixed by international law nor prevent any European power directly interested from enforcing such obligations or

[5] Carlos Alberto Silva, ed., *La Política Internacional de la Nación Argentina* (Buenos Aires: Ministerio del Interior, 1946), pp. 32–36.
[6] International American Conference, *Reports of Committees,* Vol. IV, Historical Appendix: *The Congress of 1826 at Panama and Subsequent Movements towards a Conference of American Nations,* Washington, 1890, p. 300.

from inflicting merited punishment for the breach of them. It does not contemplate any interference in the internal affairs of any American state or in the relations between it and other American states. It does not justify any attempt on our part to change the established form of government of any American state or to prevent the people of such state from altering that form according to their own will and pleasure. The rule in question has but a single purpose and object. It is that no European power or combination of European powers shall forcibly deprive an American state of the right and power of self-government and of shaping for itself its own political fortunes and destinies.[7]

Olney acknowledged the Pan-American implications of the Monroe Doctrine by declaring that "The states of America, South as well as North, by geographical proximity, by natural sympathy, by similarity of governmental constitutions, are friends and allies, commercially and politically, of the United States." But in words somewhat ominously suggesting the power potential of the Doctrine in relation to Latin America he defiantly announced that "Today the United States is practically sovereign on this continent, and its fiat is law upon the subjects to which it confines its interposition."

In pursuance of this bumptious dictum the Monroe Doctrine as a doctrine of protection for Latin America was used to justify the intervention by the United States in Cuba and the war with Spain in 1898. By doing so, the United States was charged with violating Monroe's pledge that "with the existing colonies and dependencies of any European power we have not interfered and shall not interfere." The intervention in Cuba and the annexation of Puerto Rico vividly exposed Monroe's principles as a doctrine which could be used by the United States against Spanish-speaking countries in the Western Hemisphere. In 1898 the Argentine statesman Roque Saenz Peña delivered an address which was typical of the Latin-American reaction. Excerpts from the address introduce the following collection of materials on the Monroe Doctrine.

---

[7] Clark, *Memorandum on the Monroe Doctrine*, p. 156.

The Monroe Doctrine was freely coupled with the arrangements which the United States made with Cuba during its military occupation of the island. With the defeat of Spanish arms in Cuba, it would be intolerable, declared the *New York Tribune,* "for Cuba to run heavily in debt to some European country and then have that country resort to military and naval occupation . . . to collect its claims."[8] To forestall this as well as other developments which might jeopardize the security interests of the United States, the McKinley administration defined its relations with Cuba in the Platt Amendment which Senator Orville H. Platt, the putative author of the Amendment, declared had as its objective the application of the "essence" of the Monroe Doctrine to Cuba.[9] This view was expressed also by the *San Francisco Bulletin,* which characterized the Platt Amendment as "an amplification of the Monroe Doctrine."[1]

Thus interpreted the Monroe Doctrine was finally accepted by Great Britain. Already in 1899 the nations represented at the First Hague Conference had acquiesced in a reservation by the United States embodying the substance of the Monroe Doctrine defined simply as the "traditional attitude [of the United States] toward purely American questions," and this acceptance was construed by President Theodore Roosevelt as international acceptance of the Monroe Doctrine. It should be pointed out, however, that contrary to Roosevelt's assumption the unilateral reservation by the United States delegation at The Hague could not have multilateral effect nor did the silence of the other signatory powers on this matter necessarily imply their consent to it.

The protection which the Monroe Doctrine had offered to Latin America in the nineteenth century was a protection against political interference from abroad, but at the beginning of the twentieth century the protection which seemed to be required was a protection against the economic penetration and control of the area from Europe, as alarmingly demonstrated by the debt-collecting expedition of Britain, Germany, and Italy against Venezuela in 1902. To guard the hemisphere against a European intervention which might be deemed to make future protective action by the

---

[8] February 3, 1901.
[9] Quoted in the *New York Tribune,* April 25, 1901.
[1] April 18, 1901.

United States necessary, the Argentine Foreign Minister, Luis María Drago, proposed in 1902 the principle that "the public debt should not be used as a justification for armed intervention nor for the physical occupation of the territory of the American nations by a European power." He intended that this proposal should be adopted by the other American nations and should serve as an economic corollary to the Monroe Doctrine. It would reinforce that Doctrine by restoring the principle of the equality of states in international law and assuring the independence of the states of the American hemisphere, not only against Europe but also against each other.[2]

But the relationship which the United States had established with Cuba provided it with new opportunities for investment and presaged a time in the near future when it would enter into competition with the capital-exporting nations of Europe for a privileged economic position in Latin America. To this position already assumed or to be assumed by the United States President Theodore Roosevelt considered the Drago proposal a threat, particularly if it were accepted as a multilateral or inter-American doctrine. Accordingly, in his annual message to Congress in 1904 he cited the responsibilities of the United States under the Monroe Doctrine as the reason why this country must assume "the exercise of an international police power" in the Western Hemisphere.

The United States now acquired, or at least asserted, a new power position with reference to Latin-American peoples. The new twist which Roosevelt gave to the Monroe Doctrine, making the United States and the United States alone responsible for punishing acts of "chronic wrongdoing or an impotence which results in a general loosening of the ties of civilized society" in Latin America, seemed preferable to Drago's proposal of a multilateral ban on forcible intervention by Europe in the Western Hemisphere for the collection of public debts, and it was preferred by England and other European creditors of the Latin-American nations. It was a natural and even a necessary reaction of the United States against threats to its own security occasioned by in-

[2] Luis M. Drago, *La República Argentina y el Caso de Venezuela,* pp. 1-10.

ternational developments and particularly the growing rivalry between Great Britain and Germany. Indeed Lord Salisbury may be considered the true author of the Roosevelt Corollary, for as early as 1895 he had pointed out to Olney that if the United States wished to protect the Latin-American states "from the consequences attaching to any misconduct of which they may be guilty towards other nations," it must necessarily "control the conduct of these communities." Just as identity of interest between the United States and Great Britain led to the original promulgation of the Monroe Doctrine, so the elaboration of the Doctrine in the Roosevelt Corollary in 1904 came about as the result of British instigation.

The Roosevelt Corollary to the Monroe Doctrine was used to justify military intervention in countries of Central America and the Caribbean area and the imposition later of a policy of "dollar diplomacy" upon them. It was thus used explicitly to justify the establishment and maintenance of control by the United States over governments in Latin America. It thrust upon the United States the necessity of fighting Latin Americans to compel them to allow it to protect them against Europeans. Under the Corollary the United States Senate, upon motion of Senator Henry Cabot Lodge, went so far as to adopt the so-called Magdalena Bay resolution in 1912, opposing the occupation of "any harbor or other place in the American continents" by "any corporation or association which has such a relation to another government, not American, as to give that government practical power or control for naval or military purposes." The Monroe Doctrine which had originally been a warning that America is not for Europe now was interpreted as a positive declaration that America is for the United States.

The Roosevelt Corollary and the resulting policy actions by the United States became the target of vitriolic criticism throughout Latin America and brought the Doctrine itself, which had often in the past been regarded as a shield of protection for Latin America, into disrepute. A Brazilian declaration prepared for the Fourth Inter-American Conference at Buenos Aires in 1910, lauding the principles of the Monroe Doctrine "as a permanent factor for international peace on the American continents" and expressing gratitude to the United States for that Doctrine, had to be withdrawn by its sponsor, Joaquim Nabuco, because of opposition from other American nations, implying, as it did, approval of the interventionist policy of the United States in Central America and the Caribbean.[3] The Magdalena Bay resolution was criticized in Mexico as infringing that nation's sovereign right to conclude contracts of colonization with whomever it pleased, whether nationals or foreigners, whether Englishmen, Frenchmen, Japanese, or Chinese.[4] When Theodore Roosevelt received an honorary degree from the University of Buenos Aires in 1913, he was publicly told in the address of the Dean of the Faculty of Private International Law, Estanislao S. Zeballos, that the Monroe Doctrine could not be considered to have any force south of the Gulf of Mexico and that Argentina specifically rejected it.[5] President Venustiano Carranza, in a message to the Mexican Congress, stated officially that "Mexico has not recognized and will not recognize the Monroe Doctrine, because without the consent of all the peoples of America it established a criterion and a situation on which there had been no consultations and, consequently, that Doctrine attacks the sovereignty and the independence of Mexico and would introduce and establish a guardianship over all the nations of America."[6]

In general the Roosevelt Corollary sharpened the dichotomy between the unilateralism of the Monroe Doctrine and the Pan-Americanist aspirations of the Latin-American nations which sought to give the original principles of the Doctrine hemisphere validity as a juridical element in inter-American relations. It weakened and virtually destroyed the nascent and promising Pan-Americanism which had been organized for the first time at the Inter-American Conference of 1889–1890 in Washington. Roosevelt seemed to assume, cynically wrote a distinguished Brazilian diplomat, Manuel de Oliveira Lima, that "Columbus discovered the New World for the greater profit and glory of the Anglo-

---

[3] Dexter Perkins, *A History of the Monroe Doctrine,* pp. 317–318. See also L. de Almeida Nogueira Pôrto, "Um Episódio da Doutrina de Monroe. A fórmula Nabuco na 4ª Conferência Internacional Americana," *Cultura Política,* III (June 1943), 39–42.

[4] José López-Portillo y Rojas, *La Doctrina Monroe* (Mexico, 1912).

[5] Carlos Alberto Silva, ed., *La Política Internacional de la Nación Argentina,* pp. 421–422.

[6] Quoted in Félix Pérez Porta, "La Doctrina de Monroe," p. 56.

Saxon race."[7] The relationship between the United States and Latin America under the Roosevelt Corollary was illustrated, somewhat facetiously but none the less bitterly, in a story told by the Spanish author Salvador de Madariaga about an experiment conducted by a professor to discover whether it was possible to accustom a lion and a lamb to inhabit the same cage. When he was asked whether he had been successful he replied, "Oh yes, very successful. Now and then, of course, I had to replace the lamb."

The Monroe Doctrine which had originated as a defense of the American nations against Europe had evolved in such a way as to impel the Latin-American nations to seek in Europe and after 1919 in the League of Nations a bulwark against the United States. At the Paris Peace Conference Honduras sought to have the Monroe Doctrine defined explicitly and restrictively to prevent the United States from using it for interventionist purposes, and the Honduran proposal was supported by Cuba.[8] Some Latin Americans found in the Monroe Doctrine a sufficient reason for supporting the Soviet system of government. Marxist opposition to the Doctrine was voiced in the 1920's by Vicente Lombardo Toledano, who later became secretary general of the powerful Confederation of Latin American Workers. "The Monroe Doctrine," he declared, "means that the right of interference with its weak neighbors and the privilege of exploiting them are reserved to the United States. The Monroe Doctrine has been converted into an economic declaration." He characterized it as "one aspect of Yankee imperialism."[9] Other Latin-American reactions to the Roosevelt Corollary are shown in the selections from Carlos Pereyra, José Ingenieros, Baltasar Brum, Alejandro Álvarez, Simón Planas-Suárez, Felipe Barreda, and Raúl Díez de Medina (Gaston Nerval).

The Roosevelt Corollary also became the target of opposition from anti-imperialists in the United States including

---

[7] Manuel de Oliveira Lima, *Pan-Americanismo* (*Monroe-Bolívar-Roosevelt*) (Rio de Janeiro and Paris, 1907), p. 33.

[8] George W. Baker, "Ideals and Realities in the Wilson Administration's Relations with Honduras," *The Americas*, XXI (July 1964), 12–13.

[9] Vicente Lombardo Toledano, *La Doctrina Monroe y el Movimiento Obrero* (Mexico, D.F., 1927), pp. 33, 61.

Scott Nearing, Ernest H. Gruening, Carleton Beals, and Samuel Guy Inman, some of whom went so far as to call for the abandonment not only of the Corollary but of the Doctrine itself. As representative of this viewpoint an excerpt from Hiram Bingham is included. The ablest defenses of both the Roosevelt Corollary and the Monroe Doctrine were made by Secretaries of State Elihu Root and Charles Evans Hughes, representative selections from whose speeches on this subject are also presented.

The adoption of the Good Neighbor Policy by the Herbert Hoover and Franklin D. Roosevelt administrations and the abandonment of the policy of intervention enabled the United States to rescind the Roosevelt Corollary. This Corollary was explicitly and officially dissociated from the Monroe Doctrine in a *Memorandum on the Monroe Doctrine*, which was prepared by Under Secretary of State J. Reuben Clark and published in 1930. The various interventions of the United States in Cuba, the Dominican Republic, Haiti, and Nicaragua which had been undertaken in pursuance of the Roosevelt Corollary "are not within the Doctrine as it was announced by Monroe," Clark declared in this *Memorandum*, but they could only "be accounted for as the expression of a national policy which, like the Doctrine itself, originates in the necessities of security or self-preservation." The effect of the Clark *Memorandum* was to divorce the Monroe Doctrine from its subsequent corollaries—the so-called Polk Corollary, the Roosevelt Corollary, the Lodge Corollary, and others—and to restore its original meaning.

The Monroe Doctrine had remained an exclusive policy of the United States. Former Secretary of State Elihu Root, speaking before the American Society of International Law in the early twentieth century, had declared that "since the Monroe Doctrine is a declaration based upon this nation's right of self-protection, it cannot be transmuted into a joint or common declaration by American states or any number of them." President Woodrow Wilson had ringingly declared: "The Monroe Doctrine was proclaimed by the United States on her own authority. It has always been maintained, and always will be maintained, upon her own responsibility." During the century since its announcement by Monroe the defense of the American hemisphere had not been formally recognized as a common obligation of all the American nations, although many Latin Americans had sought to counter United States imperialism under the Doctrine by reviving the suggestion which some Latin-American statesmen had made at the time of the first promulgation of the Doctrine, namely, that it should be opened to approval by all the American nations and converted into a multilateral inter-American pact. As such it would serve as a collective guaranty of the territorial inviolability of all the American nations.

While the Roosevelt Corollary was still in force the Latin Americans, partly for reasons of self-defense against the United States, sought to multilateralize the Monroe Doctrine. In the early twentieth century Brazil's Foreign Minister, Baron Rio Branco, following his country's traditional policy, suggested that the Doctrine be made a part of the international law of the American hemisphere enforceable by the cooperative action of the principal republics. Drago's proposal in 1902 was intended as a multilateral guaranty of all the American nations against debt-collecting expeditions by the European nations. His purpose, in the words of Oliveira Lima, was to "latinize Monroeism and to remove from it the taint of North American exclusivism."[1] A further elaboration of the Latin-American viewpoint on this subject was made by John Barrett, Director General of the Pan American Union, who recommended in an address in Philadelphia on April 3, 1914, that for the Monroe Doctrine should be substituted a "Pan-American Policy" which would be approved by all the American nations, which would protect the government and sovereignty of each one, and which would not carry connotations of preponderance and dictatorship by the United States. The Monroe Doctrine would be Pan-Americanized and converted into a policy of all the American nations.

In the United States President Wilson was intrigued by the idea of a Pan-Americanized Monroe Doctrine. In 1914 he went so far as to draft a Pan-American Pact pledging the American nations to "join one another in a common and mutual guaranty of territorial integrity and of political independence under republican forms of government." But this proposal, offering to multilateralize the Monroe Doctrine and at the same time, be it noted, to promote "republican" institutions throughout the hemisphere, was not ac-

---

[1] Oliveira Lima, *Pan-Americanismo,* p. 10.

cepted by the influential ABC Powers—Argentina, Brazil, and Chile—nor could it be accepted by the Latin-American nations while the United States was using the Doctrine as a pretext for imperialism. Two years later Wilson, in discussing the Monroe Doctrine, invited the American states to unite "in guaranteeing to each other absolutely political independence and territorial integrity," but he coupled his proposal with such objectionable corollaries as to render it still unacceptable to Latin America.[2]

The Monroe Doctrine was defined by Wilson in the Covenant of the League of Nations in 1919 as a "regional understanding," which it definitely was not. The acceptance of the Covenant by many of the Latin-American nations was interpreted as giving at least a measure of inter-American validity to the Monroe Doctrine though perhaps a more realistic explanation of their acceptance of it was the hope that they might find in the Covenant a counter force to use against the United States. As the United States did not join the League of Nations, it continued to treat the Monroe Doctrine as a unilateral policy obligation. The Senate Committee on Foreign Relations, in commenting on the universal treaty for the outlawry of war, the Kellogg-Briand Pact, before its ratification in 1928, explained that "The United States regards the Monroe Doctrine as a part of its national security and defense. Under the right of self-defense allowed by the treaty must necessarily be included the right to maintain the Monroe Doctrine, which is a part of our system of national defense."

Soon, however, a movement began to convert this unilateral policy into a cooperative inter-American policy. In 1931 during the Great Depression Dr. Carlos Saavedra Lamas of Argentina insisted that the Monroe Doctrine required that the United States take the lead in organizing a customs union of the American nations to defend the hemisphere against economic aggression from abroad.[3] The Good Neighbor Policy of the Hoover and Franklin D.

---

[2] Arthur S. Link, *Wilson, the New Freedom* (Princeton: Princeton University Press, 1956), pp. 324–327; and Ray Stannard Baker, *Woodrow Wilson, Life and Letters: Facing War, 1915–1917* (Garden City, N.Y.: Doubleday, 1937), pp. 82–85.

[3] Carlos Saavedra Lamas, "La Nueva Política Internacional de Hoover, su Trascendencia," *La Nación*, Buenos Aires, June 1, 1931.

Roosevelt administrations created an auspicious climate for the multilateralization of the Doctrine, restoring once more the concept of the juridical equality of all the American nations.

The liquidation of imperialism by the United States during the 1930's improved the possibility of inter-American cooperation to these ends. The United States now implemented the Clark *Memorandum* by abandoning the policy of hemispheric hegemony which it had exercised in the name of the Monroe Doctrine. The acceptance of the non-intervention principle by the United States at the Seventh Inter-American Conference at Montevideo in 1933 was hailed in Latin America as giving the *coup de grâce* to the Monroe Doctrine as a doctrine of intervention.[4]

Once again threats from outside the American hemisphere, similar to those presented by the Quadruple Alliance in 1823, seemed to call for a reaffirmation, now cooperative or collective on the part of all the American nations, of the warning against European intervention in the Americas and the imposition of alien systems there. As the Americas were confronted with the rising power of the Axis nations in the 1930's some Latin Americans saw that the Doctrine, which they had long considered a threat to their independence, might have beneficent possibilities for them, particularly if it could be given Pan-American approval. In 1936 President Alfonso López of Colombia proposed that the Monroe Doctrine be replaced with a multilateral treaty.[5] By making it a genuinely hemispheric Doctrine all the American nations would give warning to the totalitarian powers that an act of aggression against any American nation would be considered an act of aggression against all American nations. They would also counter the claims of those powers, specifically Germany, Japan, and Italy, to a right to impose their own Monroe Doctrines respectively upon Europe, Asia, and Africa. According to the German Foreign Minister von Ribbentrop, "Germany wished for nothing more in Europe than the United States had in the Western Hemisphere through

---

[4] Antonio Gómez Robledo, "La Doctrina Monroe y los Convenios de Bucareli," *Abside, Revista de Cultura Mexicana,* II (April 1938), 5–7.

[5] Department of State, Despatch 1005. Bogotá, September 29, 1936.

the Monroe Doctrine." He insisted that "Germany must have her Monroe Doctrine in Central Europe."[6]

As plans were laid for the Eighth Inter-American Conference of American States at Lima in 1938 the suggestion of a Pan-American Monroe Doctrine was made with increasing frequency in Latin America. On the eve of that conference, the Presidents of both El Salvador and Guatemala proposed to the United States that the Doctrine be transformed into a multilateral concept to counter the threat of Japanese imperialism, Italian Fascism, and German Naziism.[7] The emergence of the totalitarian regimes in Europe and Asia, declared La Nación of Santiago, Chile, had resuscitated the old Monroe Doctrine and given it new life and meaning.[8] The Monroe Doctrine, Diario Latino of San Salvador insisted, should be issued as the "American Doctrine" in which all the nations of America would give warning to the world that an act of aggression against any American nation would be considered as an act of aggression against all American nations.[9] Accordingly, at the Lima Conference all the American nations affirmed their continental solidarity and their determination to maintain it against all foreign intervention or activity that might threaten it. Confronted with a threat similar to that which had inspired the Monroe Doctrine in 1823, they agreed collectively to safeguard the hemisphere not just against physical aggression but also against subversive ideologies.

As the threat from the Axis powers became more menacing, the foreign ministers of all the American nations met at Panama immediately after the outbreak of World War II and agreed to exclude belligerent action from the American hemisphere. The United States had meanwhile unilaterally extended the area of the hemisphere which was covered by the Monroe Doctrine. Secretaries of State Daniel Webster and James G. Blaine had long before thrown the mantle of its protection over the Hawaiian Islands which were subse-

---

[6] Conversation with Under Secretary of State Sumner Welles, on March 1, 1940, as reported in Sumner Welles, The Time for Decision (New York and London: Harper and Brothers, 1944), pp. 95–96.

[7] Department of State, Despatch 539, Guatemala, March 17, 1938; and Despatch 696, Guatemala, September 24, 1938.

[8] April 22, 1938.

[9] Department of State, Despatch 539, Guatemala, March 17, 1938.

quently annexed to the United States. President Franklin D. Roosevelt, as the Axis menace threatened, extended the same protection to both Canada and Greenland.

Not until after the outbreak of the war in Europe in 1939 did it become possible to give hemispheric affirmation to all the principles of the Monroe Doctrine. Monroe had made plain in his message of 1823 that "with the existing colonies or dependencies of any European power we have not interfered and shall not interfere." But even at that time it had become the settled policy of the United States to oppose the transfer of any colony in America from one European power to another. As early as 1808 President Thomas Jefferson and his Cabinet had expressed their disapproval of the rumored transfer of Cuba from weak Spain to a stronger nation, in that case England, and warned Spain against making any deals in American real estate. This "no-transfer" principle, based upon the protection of the peace and security of the United States, was confirmed by a Congressional resolution in 1811 relating to Spanish Florida. It formed an important element in the historic background of the policy pronouncement which Monroe made in 1823 but was not included as a principle in the original Monroe Doctrine. It was later reaffirmed by President Ulysses Grant in 1870. The retention of such colonies by European powers, it was sometimes argued, made those powers American states for the purposes of the Monroe Doctrine, but this argument was refuted by Secretary of State Olney in his correspondence with Lord Salisbury in 1895. If it were accepted, said Olney, "not only would every European power now having a South [Latin] American colony be enabled to extend its possessions on this continent indefinitely, but any other European power might also do the same by first taking pains to procure a fraction of South [Latin] American soil by voluntary cession."

After Germany's occupation of Paris in June 1940 the United States, as well as other nations of the Americas, became alarmed at the prospect that the victorious Nazis might take over France's possessions in the Western Hemisphere. To forestall such action, President Roosevelt in 1940 notified Germany that the United States, "in accordance with its traditional policy relating to the Western Hemisphere, . . . would not recognize any transfer, and would not acquiesce in any attempt to transfer any geographic region of the Western Hemisphere from one non-American power to another non-American power." This policy statement was a prelude to the adoption by the foreign ministers of the American nations, in their Second Meeting at Havana in July 1940, of the Act of Havana in which they arranged to establish a provisional administration over colonial possessions of European powers in the Western Hemisphere if those possessions should be threatened or attacked by a European belligerent. This Act was supplemented by a convention providing for the establishment of an Inter-American Commission on Territorial Administration to supervise the management of such colonial possessions. Thus the American governments for the first time gave collective confirmation to the no-transfer principle and arranged to enforce it through collaborative action.

Also for the first time the American nations agreed at Havana that any attempt by a non-American nation against the territory, sovereignty, or political independence of an American nation "shall be considered as an act of aggression" against all the American nations. Resistance to foreign intervention in the American hemisphere was finally recognized as a common responsibility of all the nations of the hemisphere rather than the unilateral obligation of one. Under the grinding exigencies of World War II all the elements of the Monroe Doctrine were thus accepted as a collective obligation of all the American nations, but not under the name of the Monroe Doctrine. The American nations made plain their united opposition (1) to the transfer of European colonies in America from one non-American power to another non-American power, (2) to European interference with their political system, which they defined as "the common inter-American democratic ideal," and (3) to European territorial expansion in America.

After the Japanese assault on Pearl Harbor in December 1941 the foreign ministers of all the American nations met at Rio de Janeiro and elaborated their definition of the second principle by undertaking to "prevent subversive activities of nationals of non-American countries" in the American hemisphere. Meanwhile both Germany and Japan were justifying their careers of conquest in Europe and Asia respectively with the Monroe Doctrine, arguing that they were only trying to establish the same kind of spheres of influence in those areas as the United States had established in the Americas.

All the principles incorporated in the Monroe Doctrine were thus transmuted into a joint or common declaration in these various inter-American agreements, summarized above. As was the case of the original enunciation of the Monroe Doctrine in 1823 and the Roosevelt Corollary in 1904, the Pan-Americanization of the Doctrine in the agreements of World War II came about as the result of the identification of the interests of the United States with those of Britain. A Pan-American plan of hemispheric defense was developed to protect the American nations against England's enemies, who were deemed also to be threatening the Americas.

But this was not done without opposition from Latin-American nationalists. "Monroeism," bitterly complained the Mexican intellectual and political leader José Vasconcelos, "was not abolished by the policy of the Good Neighbor, which is the supposed 'New Deal' of Pan-Americanism. . . . Far from being dead, Monroeism is still very much alive and active."[1] In the opinion of the acidulous Argentine critic Carlos Ibarguren, the hemispheric security system was imposed by the United States and represented "the apogee of that policy of continental absorption which began to appear in 1823 in Monroe's famous message."[2] But the acceptance of the principles of the Monroe Doctrine by all the American nations, though it could be construed as logically fulfilling the Pan-American implications of the Doctrine, had the effect, from the Seventh Inter-American Conference onward, of affirming the right of each American nation to its own integrity and sovereignty in relation to every other nation whether American or foreign and so has contributed to the strengthening of the forces of nationalism in the Americas which has occurred since World War II.

The inter-American pledges were converted into a regional security system for the American hemisphere in the Act of Chapultepec, which was signed at the Mexico City Conference on War and Peace in 1945. Such regional security arrangements were recognized in the Charter of the

---

[1] "El Monroísmo en Acción," *Hoy*, Mexico City, June 4, 1938.
[2] Carlos Ibarguren, *De Monroe a la Buena Vecindad: Trayectoria de un Imperialismo* (Buenos Aires, 1946).

United Nations, drawn up at San Francisco later in the same year, but the Charter, unlike the Covenant of the League of Nations a quarter of a century earlier, did not specifically mention the Monroe Doctrine. Nevertheless by giving its approval to regional systems the Charter, in a sense, gave universal recognition to "Monroeism." The conditions and obligations of the Western Hemisphere regional security system were defined in the Inter-American Treaty of Reciprocal Assistance, the so-called Pact of Rio de Janeiro, in 1947, which declared that "an armed attack by any state against an American state shall be considered as an attack against all the American states" and pledged each one of them "to assist in meeting the attack in the exercise of the inherent right of individual or collective self-defense."

In summary, the no-transfer principle, which antedated Monroe's original pronouncement and which was later added to the Monroe Doctrine, was Pan-Americanized in the Act of Havana of 1940. The first and second principles of the original Monroe Doctrine, namely, those opposing European colonization in the American continents and the extension of a non-American system and non-American control over the nations of the Western Hemisphere, were Pan-Americanized finally in the Pact of Rio de Janeiro in 1947. With the emergence, or rather, the clearer appreciation of the threat of Soviet communism after 1945 the inter-American obligation of collective defense was made explicit as against communism in the Act of Caracas, adopted at the Tenth Inter-American Conference in 1954, which declared that "the domination or control of the political institutions of any American state by the international Communist movement, extending to this hemisphere the political system of an extracontinental power, would constitute a threat to the sovereignty and political independence of the American states." So, in phrases reminiscent of the Monroe Doctrine, the basis was laid for united Pan-American action against the international Communist movement as a non-American political and conspiratorial system. But this action was not taken without considerable opposition from those Latin-American nations which regarded it as antithetic to their cherished principle of non-intervention.

The Monroe Doctrine in all its elements thus was given continental or multilateral expression and as such came to be regarded as virtually synonymous with Pan-Americanism. Elihu Root had declared that "the Monroe Doctrine . . . cannot be transmuted into a joint or common declaration by American states or any number of them." But it has been so transmuted, not by name but in all its essential principles. Resistance to threats from abroad against the peace and safety of the peoples of the American hemisphere has been made a common obligation of all the American nations. But in the process the nations of Latin America, determined to protect themselves from intervention, have also bound themselves to oppose intervention by each other, including the United States. They have agreed that every threat to their independence, whether coming from inside or outside the American hemisphere, must be resisted.

But were Monroeism and Pan-Americanism identical? And did the United States by merging its national voice with the voice of the entire continent abandon the Monroe Doctrine? Is it still a national policy, the "ark of the covenant" in foreign affairs? In 1944 former Under Secretary of State Sumner Welles wrote that "In the entire history of the United States since 1823 there has been but one basis of our foreign policy which has been supported by all the people of this country and to which all political parties have consistently adhered, and that is the Monroe Doctrine."[3] Is this still true? What effect has the Pan-Americanization of the principles of the Doctrine had upon its status both in the United States and in Latin America? Does the Doctrine remain, since all its principles have been transformed into an international engagement of all the American nations, a national policy of the United States? Does the fact that it has not been internationalized by name weaken it as a unilateral doctrine to be invoked, as it was originally invoked, for the defense of the United States?

The history of the Monroe Doctrine before World War I was marked by an unfortunate ambivalence between, on the one hand, the defense of the hemisphere and, on the other, the hegemony of the United States in it, and since World War II by an ambivalence between a continental view and a world view of the interests of the United States. The Monroe Doctrine has long been identified with a policy of isola-

---

[3] Sumner Welles, *The Time for Decision,* p. 401.

tion of the American continents from the rest of the world and opposed by its very nature to internationalism. But the involvement of the United States in two World Wars and its assumption of world-wide commitments, including the establishment of military, naval, and air bases in many parts of the non-American world, have destroyed the fundamental condition upon which the principles of the Monroe Doctrine rested, namely abstention of the United States from participation "in the wars of the European powers" and noninterference in the internal concerns of those powers. Can the United States logically and in good conscience oppose foreign encroachments upon American shores when at the same time it is intervening beyond the shores of other continents, African, European, and Asiatic? Can it protect the Americas from the balance-of-power system of foreign nations while itself engaging in balance-of-power politics on a world-wide scale? Under these circumstances has the Monroe Doctrine, as a policy of isolation and neutrality in relation to the Old World, lost its *raison d'être?*

Monroe, of course, did not envisage the time when the United States would defend itself with armies on the Rhine and the Yalu. Since World War II the doctrine of the two spheres or, better, the two hemispheres—an Eastern and a Western—has given way to a doctrine of an Atlantic community embodied in the NATO Pact of 1949 and the even broader doctrine of a division between the Communist world and the so-called free world, the latter including countries as remote from the Americas as Greece, Turkey, and Laos. The United States in accepting this conception of its defense interests has relegated the Latin-American nations to a secondary or even tertiary role in its foreign policy and, according to one view, no longer can base policy upon the isolation and protection of its interests in the Western Hemisphere. As the Monroe Doctrine rested on the United States's conception of its peculiar defense needs in the Western Hemisphere that Doctrine is no longer useful or even existent.

Many Latin Americans have responded coldly to the United States's alarms over the menace of communism and have regarded the United States's efforts to counteract it through hemispheric action as a greater threat to their independence. They have shown considerable doubt as to whether communism is truly an alien system which aims at establishing control over American governments and constitutes a threat to their security. In addition, the construction given to the Monroe Doctrine by Olney and Theodore Roosevelt is repeatedly used against the United States by Soviet propaganda directed at Latin America. Since the acceptance of the principles of the Monroe Doctrine by the other American nations, United States policy makers and agencies of public opinion have been disinclined to cite the Doctrine as a policy of national defense. They have been inhibited by the stigma that still attaches to it as a doctrine of United States imperialism. It is considered an unmentionable word in inter-American relations, and an appeal to it is often followed by adverse emotional reactions. Moreover, the multilateralization of the Monroe Doctrine has tended to limit the freedom of action of public officials in relation to national defense. As an alternative defense measure some influential officials and newspapers, judging that unilateral measures are no longer appropriate in the modern world, are inclined to place reliance upon international agencies, such as the Organization of American States, NATO, and the United Nations, instead of the Monroe Doctrine.

But this view is challenged by those who insist that the Western Hemisphere still has peculiar defense requirements which must be safeguarded and which must be safeguarded primarily by the United States acting in its own interest and in accordance with the basic principles of the Monroe Doctrine. That Doctrine remains for the United States a doctrine of self-defense; in essence it is inseparable from the United States and from its republican system of government. The impasse between Soviet Russia and the United States which has developed since World War II arises from the fact that, as in 1823, each nation is engaged in defending its national interest by opposing alien systems of government. If all of Europe should fall under Communist domination, a situation would again be created similar to that of 1823 requiring the defense of the Western Hemisphere. And, even more alarmingly, the long arm of the Soviets has already reached into the Western Hemisphere in clear defiance of the Monroe Doctrine.

Since World War II the Monroe Doctrine has been

openly challenged by the pro-Soviet actions of the Jacobo Arbenz regime in Guatemala (1951–1954) and the Fidel Castro regime in Cuba (1959–   ). The "intrusion of Soviet despotism" into Guatemala was denounced by Secretary of State John Foster Dulles as "a direct challenge to our Monroe Doctrine, the first and most fundamental of our foreign policies." It led to the adoption of the anti-Communist declaration at Caracas in 1954 and to the summoning of a meeting of foreign ministers which, however, lost its reason for convening when the Arbenz government was overthrown by Colonel Castillo Armas in 1954, with some help from the United States.

After the Castro government had established itself in Cuba Premier Nikita Khrushchev announced that the Monroe Doctrine had "died a natural death." In reply the State Department reaffirmed the Monroe Doctrine, declaring that its "principles are as valid today as they were in 1823 when the Doctrine was proclaimed," and, as it pointed out, these principles are now "supported by the inter-American security system through the Organization of American States." In a news conference soon afterward, however, President Dwight D. Eisenhower excluded from the purview of the Doctrine Communist-dominated governments in the American hemisphere that come to power by the free election of their people.[4]

The threat of the Castro government to the security of the United States and of the American hemisphere as a whole became clear in 1962 when Castro made an outright military alliance with Soviet Russia in pursuance of which he received from Khrushchev assurances that Russia would fortify Cuba as a military base. Russia subsequently sent to Cuba various types of missiles as well as jet planes, anti-aircraft rockets, radar equipment, torpedo boats firing atomic weapons, tanks, and a multitude of "technical experts" to train Cubans in the use of these weapons. Not since the French invasion of Mexico in the 1860's had a foreign power ventured to mount so powerful a military stronghold in the American hemisphere.

---

[4] President Dwight D. Eisenhower, News Conference, August 10, 1960, *Public Papers of the Presidents of the United States: Dwight D. Eisenhower, 1960–61*, Washington, Government Printing Office, pp. 622–623.

In the various official exchanges on the situation created by the Castro regime in Cuba neither the Eisenhower nor the Kennedy administrations explicitly invoked the Monroe Doctrine, though Kennedy explained in a news conference on August 29, 1962, that his administration was defending the Monroe Doctrine by seeking to "isolate the Communist menace in Cuba," thus testifying to the continued vitality of the Doctrine in United States public opinion. *Time* magazine in its issue of September 21, 1962, characterized the Doctrine as "plain and solid and durable as a slab of bronze," and proposals were made in Congress that the United States specifically invoke the Monroe Doctrine and place an embargo on shipments of Soviet military materials and personnel to Cuba. Under pressure of this sort President Kennedy announced in an address on October 22, 1962, that "It shall be the policy of this nation to regard any nuclear missile launched from Cuba against any nation in the Western Hemisphere as an attack by the Soviet Union on the United States, requiring a full retaliatory response upon the Soviet Union." In thus specifying the nature of the reprisal to be taken by the United States he added, in this so-called Kennedy Corollary to the Monroe Doctrine, a sanction not included in Monroe's original pronouncement.

In subsequent negotiations with Khrushchev the United States considerably moderated this policy threat. It agreed, in exchange for a concession by Russia allowing on-the-spot surveillance of Soviet withdrawal of "offensive" weapons from Cuba, not to invade the island nor assist any other American nation to do so. But for Russia's rejection of this surveillance the United States would have imposed upon itself the very self-denying limitation which Adams had carefully avoided in 1823. The Monroe Doctrine had been reversed, as it were, to declare in effect that "any interposition from the countries of the Western Hemisphere for the purpose of controlling the destiny of a Communist state in the Western Hemisphere would constitute a threat to the security of the Soviet Union."[5]

This concession was probably deemed to be necessary because of the extension of United States security actions

---

[5] Robert D. Crane, "The Cuban Crisis: A Strategic Analysis of American and Soviet Policy," *Orbis*, VI (Winter 1963), 548.

into areas bordering the Soviet Union in contravention of the third principle of the original Monroe Doctrine. While the United States maintains military bases and forces in countries bordering the Soviet Union, how can it, consistently with the Monroe Doctrine, deny a similar right to Russia in the case of Cuba? Meanwhile the Monroe Doctrine whether as a policy of the United States alone or as a policy supported by all the American nations is repeatedly cited by the exiles from Castro's Cuba as requiring the use of force, either by the United States or by the nations of the entire hemisphere, to destroy Castro's Communist regime. "The Monroe Doctrine is still in force," declares Dr. Carlos Márquez Sterling, former President of the Cuban Constitutional Convention of 1940. "It was born out of the opposition to the enemy of those times. It serves equally well against the enemy of our times."[6]

To reassert the Monroe Doctrine as a policy of the United States particularly in relation to Cuba, a Committee for the Monroe Doctrine was organized in October 1962 with headquarters in New York. It was headed by Captain Eddie Rickenbacker and composed of many prominent citizens of the United States. It has waged a strenuous campaign against the Kennedy-Johnson policy toward Cuba arguing for strong action in defense of the Monroe Doctrine. The members are convinced that, in the words of one of their publications, "Either we will go forward to a firm reiteration and implementation of the Monroe Doctrine or, in failure of will, we are likely to see all Latin America passing irretrievably under the sway of Khrushchev or Tito communism." The United States, faced with this dilemma, "cannot forswear its inherent right of self-defense. That right is written into the Monroe Doctrine." While the Castro regime remains entrenched in Cuba and in alliance with Soviet Russia the Committee complains that "the Monroe Doctrine has been junked," and they have asked Congress to "resolve that the Monroe Doctrine continues to be a basic plank of American foreign policy."[7]

---

[6] Carlos Márquez Sterling, "La Doctrina Monroe," *Hablemos Magazine, Revista Dominical de los Diarios de América,* New York, June 30, 1963, pp. 16–17.

[7] Committee for the Monroe Doctrine, "Cuba and the Monroe Doctrine," radio address by Eddie Rickenbacker, December 2, 1962.

But proposals for implementation of the Monroe Doctrine along these lines in Cuba are obliged to compete with problems in other and more remote crisis spots around the world and with alternative measures of national defense which are not associated with the Monroe Doctrine. Moreover, although Monroe had the backing of the British when he announced the Doctrine and Theodore Roosevelt carried out British policy in announcing his Corollary, the United States has lacked British support in dealing with the Castro problem in Cuba. It has also been inhibited by disagreements as to both methods and objectives among the members of the Organization of American States.

The Monroe Doctrine has been cited often as requiring the eviction of European powers from their colonial holdings in America. The United States, in expelling Spain from Cuba and Puerto Rico in 1898, established a precedent which has nourished the hope among Latin Americans for the expulsion of other European nations from their colonial dominions in the Americas. The continuance of European colonialism in the Falkland (Malvinas) Islands claimed by Argentina, and in Belize claimed by Guatemala, and retention of territories in the Guianas by the British, French, and Dutch have been criticized as aggression against the hemisphere which necessitates action under the Monroe Doctrine.[8]

Opponents of continued European colonialism in the Americas derive support from Olney's dictum to Salisbury in 1895, interpreting the Monroe Doctrine, that "three thousand miles of intervening ocean make any permanent political union between a European and an American state unnatural and inexpedient" and that such a union inevitably introduces the clash of European politics into the American hemisphere. Since World War II the continuance of European as well as United States colonialism has been vigorously challenged by Argentina, Guatemala, and Venezuela, the last-named of which occasionally asserts claims to part or all of British Guiana. In the post-war Latin-American drive to oust the colonial powers from their possessions in the American hemisphere the position of the United States in Puerto Rico has also been assailed.

---

[8] Vicente Sáenz, *Hispanoamérica contra el Coloniaje*, 3rd edition (Mexico, D.F.: Editorial América Nueva, 1956), pp. 105–106, 111–116.

The American nations represented at the Ninth Inter-American Conference at Bogotá in 1948 adopted a resolution declaring that "it is a just aspiration of the American Republics that colonialism and the occupation of American territories by extracontinental countries should be brought to an end." Pursuant to this resolution Guatemala, having a special interest in expelling the British from Belize, insisted that the Monroe Doctrine be invoked to make "all European colonialists now holding American territory abandon the hemisphere once and for all." "This," declared President Miguel Ydígoras Fuentes of Guatemala in 1963, "is the consolidation of the Monroe Doctrine and must also include the present case of Cuba."[9]

Since the time of Calhoun the Monroe Doctrine has often been pronounced dead, solemn requiems have been said over it, and it has been repeatedly buried, but because it is basically a doctrine of the defense of the United States it has reappeared in an astonishing number of reincarnations. "The Monroe Doctrine," declared President Grover Cleveland," is important to our peace and safety as a nation and is essential to the integrity of our free institutions and the tranquil maintenance of our distinctive form of government. . . . It cannot become obsolete," he declared, "while our republic endures." And former President Theodore Roosevelt asserted in a speech in Santiago, Chile, in 1914: "If anyone states that it [the Monroe Doctrine] is dead, I shall ask him if this means that, from now forward, the Old World powers may acquire territories by conquest or colonization in these continents. Only he who thinks thus can pretend that the Monroe Doctrine is dead." The persistence of the doctrine of the two spheres was attested much later by Secretary of State John Foster Dulles when he declared, "there exists among the American states some sentiment of solidarity which sets them apart from other nations of the world."

To strengthen this sentiment of solidarity is one purpose of the aid program of the United States in Latin America, as embodied first in the Point Four operation and after 1961 in

---

[9] Miguel Ydígoras Fuentes, "The Consolidation of the Monroe Doctrine, as proposed to the peoples of the Americas by the Republic of Guatemala in Central America through the offices of the Organization of American States (O.A.S.), Guatemala, C.A., January 1, 1963."

the Alliance for Progress. The aid program has given the
Monroe Doctrine a new aspect; it is intended to counter a
modern form of aggression against the hemisphere from
abroad, namely Communist subversion. But it is quite con-
sistent with the Monroe Doctrine, which, it should be
emphasized, threw the weight of the United States against
the extension to the American nations of a foreign "system"
for the purpose of controlling their destiny. The Pan-Americanization of the principle opposing the introduction of a
foreign system into the Americas for such a purpose has, in
reality, only served to strengthen the Monroe Doctrine and
makes it more obligatory than before for each nation, including the United States, to enforce it.

The sentiment of solidarity in defense of the national
interests of each American nation is suggested in the principles of the Monroe Doctrine. But the Monroe Doctrine as
such is unilateral; Pan-Americanism on the other hand is
multilateral. The Monroe Doctrine itself, being essentially
and completely a unilateral policy of the United States,
cannot be Pan-Americanized. Its original purpose was the
defense of the United States, not the defense of the hemisphere. It does not cease to exist by being multilateralized,
but it is transformed into Pan-Americanism which may or
may not, depending upon circumstances, be equated with
the security of the United States. For this reason the Monroe Doctrine is not and cannot be made an all-American
doctrine.

Looking back over this long discussion of the Monroe
Doctrine, it seems clear that Monroe's declaration did not
violate any principles of international law. On the contrary
it rested, as Secretary of State Charles Evans Hughes explained in 1923, "upon the right of every sovereign state to
protect itself by preventing a condition of affairs in which it
will be too late to protect itself." It relied also in effect, as
noted above, upon the principle of *uti possidetis* long recognized in international law. The Monroe Doctrine as a unilateral policy of the United States is not international law,
but it asserts principles which have been incorporated in the
international law of the Americas. The acceptance of the
principles of the Doctrine by the other American nations has
transferred those principles into the domain of law without,
however, detracting from their validity and force in the

domain of United States politics. In this view the Monroe Doctrine remains a political instrument to be resorted to, when necessary, unilaterally by the United States.

Such was the interpretation some commentators placed upon President Lyndon Johnson's dispatch of U.S. Marines in late April 1965 to the Dominican Republic, which was, as he charged, threatened with a Communist takeover. They viewed it as unilateral action implementing the Monroe Doctrine. President Johnson chose to consider this action as justified, at least in part, by accepted principles of inter-American security. "The American nations cannot, must not, and will not permit the establishment of another Communist government in the Western Hemisphere," he declared in a television address on May 2. Since, as he explained in a subsequent press conference, "the nations of this hemisphere have repeatedly made it clear that the principles of communism are incompatible with the principles of the inter-American system," he disclaimed any possibility of a new "Johnson Doctrine."

As the Monroe Doctrine obviously does not encompass the whole of United States policy toward Europe, equally obviously it does not encompass the whole of United States policy toward Latin America. It is essentially a doctrine of the United States versus Europe and only incidentally concerns itself with relations between the United States and Latin America. And in this latter area of inter-American relations it does not embrace all the policy possibilities available to the United States. It does not, for example, exhaust its security obligations nor inhibit the United States from taking whatever actions are dictated by those obligations. But any unilateral action taken in pursuance of the Monroe Doctrine which ignores or violates inter-American law, whether or not resulting from the Doctrine, must be taken only after due consideration is given to the consequences of such action. No justification can be found in the Monroe Doctrine for the supposition that all the relations between the United States and the Latin-American nations are subsumed in the Doctrine or that all phases of the Doctrine lead inevitably into Pan-Americanism.

These and other fundamental points in the interpretation and application of the Monroe Doctrine are discussed pro and con in the selections that follow.

A DOCTRINE
OF INTERVENTION

Roque Saenz Peña

At the time of the original enunciation of the Monroe
Doctrine and for many years thereafter it was treated
as a doctrine of non-intervention in Latin America.
Administrations in Washington refrained from interfering in the affairs of the independent Latin-American
nations and accepted Monroe's dictum that "with the
existing colonies or dependencies of any European
power [in Latin America] we have not interfered and
shall not interfere." But when the Polk administration
went to war against Mexico in 1846, it abandoned the
non-intervention principle in favor of conquest, and the
declaration of war against Spain by the McKinley administration in 1898 "liberated" Spain's colonies Cuba
and Puerto Rico. This latter action, depriving Spain of
her last colonial possessions in the Western Hemisphere, was criticized in Latin America and particularly in a notable and emotional address by an Argentine political leader, Roque Saenz Peña, delivered in
Buenos Aires on May 2, 1898, under the sponsorship of
the Spanish Club of Buenos Aires.

As an Argentine delegate to the First Inter-American

Roque Saenz Peña, *España y Estados Unidos, Función dada en el
Teatro de la Victoria el 2 de Mayo de 1898 bajo el patrocinio del Club
Español de Buenos Aires, a beneficio de la Suscripción Nacional
Española* . . . (Buenos Aires: Companía Sud-Americana de Billetes
de Banco, 1898), pp. 13–19. Translated by the editor.

Congress in 1889–1890 Saenz Peña had repudiated Monroe's principle "America for the Americans" in favor of the principle "America for humanity." He was elected President of Argentina in 1910 and died in office four years later.

The Doctrine of President Monroe, contained in the message of December [1823], was a declaration against intervention; but that declaration contained mental reservations which rendered its objectives doubtful and its effects pernicious; in principle it condemned European interventions, but in fact it did not oppose American interventions, which means that it is not a general, scientific doctrine with unity of concept and principle but rather a national, specific act. It appears to the world as the whim of a strong and invincible power, for it must be noted that the arrogances of the White House were sustained by British squadrons and the backing of the Canning ministry.

That Doctrine in my opinion is the cause and origin of the present perversions of public law. The Mackinley [sic] doctrine is simply the latest chapter in the Monroe Doctrine and the Polk doctrine; they are not three doctrines, they are three acts sanctifying a single usurpation: the intervention of the United States in the destinies and life of the peoples of the Americas.

When the divine-right governments of Europe were threatening to spread their system over this continent, the declaration of the United States was justified on political grounds, however much justification it may have lacked on juridical grounds: it was an arbitrary act opposing an illegal act. But in the present posture of law, diplomacy, and humanity both the arbitrary and the illegal ought to disappear. No American nation exists nor ever has existed with sufficient political and international capacity to assume to represent the entire continent and to serve as the spokesman for its free peoples; just as there never has existed a single foreign chancellery for the New World, so also there is no single sovereign for the hemisphere.

President Monroe's claims to authority were not only debatable: they were fictitious because no American state had delegated nor alienated its authority to determine its relations with other nations of the world. The warnings which Monroe directed toward Europe were not ratified by the new nations in whose name he spoke and whose destinies he undertook to dispose of; the so-called Doctrine did not emerge from the halls of Congress but remained an internal action without either diplomatic or international ramifications. The essence of that Doctrine in fact was unacceptable not only to Europe, where it evoked protests from Russia and later from Great Britain, but also to the free nations of this continent. To condemn European interventions while at the same time reserving an American right of intervention and to exercise such a right unilaterally and without consultations is not in fact to censure intervention but rather to claim a monopoly of it. Lawrence has said very appropriately: "There is not a public law for Europe and a private law for America: the law of nations is of universal application throughout Christendom, and acts which are committed in the individual and selfish interest of a nation are not principles nor do they constitute a doctrine."

The position of the Latin-American states *vis à vis* a government which has taken over the officious management of the New World in relation to Europe is to ask: From what source did you obtain your solicitorship? Whence came your police authority and your inquisitorial powers over independent states which are no less inviolable than those of Europe? Will we have to search for them in the right of primogeniture, which is an accident of birth rather than law? Will we find them in the right of geographical proximity, which is an accident of nature and not reason?

We will have to conclude finally and emphatically that force creates doctrine, that the army establishes rights.

The Latin-American republics must vindicate, both by honor and title, the generous force of a new doctrine—a doctrine which was consecrated by Bolívar in convoking and organizing the Panama Congress. Bolívar possessed a sure insight into the future and was able to foresee from a distance that [Monroe's] message of December had its Achilles heel. . . .

The theme which Bolívar stressed in convoking that Congress consecrated the doctrine of non-intervention not against Europe but against every foreign power; that was the doctrine in its juridical and universal character; that was the true policy to which the peoples of the Americas aspired in order to become sovereign and free not only in relation to Europe but in relation to all nations. But that redemptive doctrine of free nations which clipped the wings of the eagles of the Capitol provoked the discontent of the Cabinet in Washington to such an extent that the United States was not represented at Panama; one of its delegates arrived late and ill, and the other never arrived because he died on the way. Bolívar proposed not only to establish the true doctrine but also to elevate the stature of these republics by correcting the inert plasticity to which they had been reduced by the message of December 2; he wished to give them political capacity so that they could act of their own accord and strength when deciding their destinies, or speaking in the name of America, or working under the care of the United States.

The Federal Congress [in Washington] rejected the proposals of that Congress, repudiating all political solidarity with the states of the South which it could neither support nor control. . . .

The subsequent actions of the United States toward the Latin-American peoples have not been more friendly or more considerate. The Washington conference of 1890, which was summoned to create happy relations among the American nations, served only to widen the distances between them and to accentuate antagonisms. It was not called to modify nor to perfect the bases of public law; there no mention was made of continental political interests nor of the generous ideals which should be shared in common. Governments and men live distrustful of each other and act only for their own advantage; it is not a question of rights nor even of fraternity: they search for consumer markets for protected products, exchanging hides for petroleum and manufactures for rubber or coffee.

The commercial link is broken by the failure of the continental bloc which was devised to counteract the commerce of Europe; Americanism has once more collapsed into a disparate thing of mountains and rivers.

I have spoken imprecisely: it is being reborn and is complicated by arbitrary interventions, as, for example, without any doubt, was applied in Venezuela, and was imposed in 1879 to end the war between Peru, Chile, and Bolivia. . . .

A SPANISH VIEW

Manuel de la Plaza

The defeat of Spain by the United States and the wresting from her of her colonies Cuba and Puerto Rico in the Western Hemisphere in 1898 ended Spain's empire in America and was one of a series of events which marked the evolution of the United States into an imperialist power. The expansion of the United States at the expense of Spanish-speaking countries under the pretext of the Monroe Doctrine was bitterly criticized by a Spanish writer, Manuel de la Plaza, in a long article, "La Doctrina de Monroe," published in three parts, which concluded as follows:

The fall of Napoleon and the coalition of great powers which proclaimed the principle of intervention at the Congresses of the Holy Alliance as a decisive force which would assure the maintenance of absolutist regimes furnished the pretext by which the United States, fearing European intervention, hastened to declare by the voice of Monroe the principles which have since been applied capriciously by the defenders of the Doctrine. And if this [Doctrine] is not

Manuel de la Plaza, "La Doctrina de Monroe," *Revista General de Legislación y Jurisprudencia*, Madrid, CVIII (1906), 229–240; 356–368; 479–496. The above excerpt is taken from pp. 493–496. Translated by the editor.

acceptable in principle—neither in the matter of colonization for the reasons which we have given, nor in the matter
of intervention because though it was based on a just principle it has not been carried out in practice—much less can
it be accepted in its applications, as we have been able to
prove in the course of this work.

The South American states which received with signs of
unusual joy the declaration of the President of the United
States, believing that it signalled for them an era of prosperity caused by their alliance with the Great Republic of
the North, have had time to be convinced of the contrary.

They could have reached that conclusion after the first
Congress of Panama. That liberty of action which the North
Americans claimed for themselves while they waited for
events produced the unexpected annexation of Texas, gave
rise to similar proposals as to the island of Santo Domingo,
and is the cause of the situation in which they have been
placed by the treaties of Bogotá [1846 and 1900], the
Clayton-Bulwer [1850], and the recent one with Panama
[1903], extending their powerful dominion by means of
these great abuses. Aside from the justice of the Venezuelan
case they imposed their mediation upon England in the time
of Cleveland, and have directed toward Spain a series of
insults, causing us to lose the last remnants of our past
greatness in an unjust, cruel, and treacherous war.

Now we can show with complete clarity why the North
Americans see that their desires were so well interpreted by
Monroe and why all the Presidents of the United States
have regarded his Doctrine as a policy guide. The words
"America for the Americans," which have always been considered as the formula that embodies the entire content of
the message, have been replaced by these other much more
exact words: "America for the Americans—of the north."

The danger which this phrase embodies is not new; it was
predicted by a minister of Louis XVI (M. de Vergennes)
who said to Lord Stremont [Stormont] when the United
States separated from England: "I see the results of that
independence to which your colonies aspire; they will want
to have squadrons, and as they do not lack any resources
they will be able to oppose all the navies of Europe and to
conquer our islands." And speaking of the dangers which
would result from the independence of the young Repub-

lic, he said: "It is certain that these results (coming from the separation) will not occur tomorrow and that neither you, My Lord, nor I will see them; but though they may be more or less distant in time they are none the less certain. A short-sighted politician can rejoice at the evils which afflict a rival nation without thinking of what will happen tomorrow. But for him who looks further and weighs the future the thing that is now happening in America is a lamentable fact, the consequences of which will affect all the nations which have colonies in the New World."

However many are the abuses occasioned by the intervention of the United States of America still worse is the turn which it has been taking for some time. Beginning with the annexation of the Hawaiian Islands the North Americans, having increased their territory at the expense of the European colonies and of the American republics, began to expand their domination into the ocean through a new application of the Monroe Doctrine. Our Cuban war, which has given them the Philippines, has been the means by which they have asserted their right, alleging their proximity to China, to join the concert of Europe.

At the same time England, which had been driven into a course of "imperialism" by commercial competition, now thought of her *brothers* in America in order to fulfill their common destiny; the offer which the North Americans initially rejected because living an abundant life they feared that they would lose their freedom of action was gradually accepted, giving a threatening character to intervention in North America.

In a recent work of the present President of the United States [Theodore Roosevelt], this point was made in the following words:

Lord Salisbury at first put in emphatic words his refusal in any way to recognize the Monroe Doctrine as part of the law of nations or as binding upon Great Britain. Most British statesmen and publicists followed his lead; but recently a goodly number have shown an inclination to acquiesce in the views of Lord Salisbury's colleague, Mr. Chamberlain, who announces, with bland indifference to the expressed opinion of his nominal chief, that England does recognize the existence of the Monroe Doctrine and never thought of ignoring it.

The importance of these words just quoted is clearly apparent at first reading. England has now found the support for her commerce and the United States the means of meddling in European affairs. Good proof of it is the aid which England gave in disguised form to the North Americans in our war with the colonies.

And imperialism, that theory which, according to Bérard, will transform the world "into an immense cooperative society of production and consumption from which England as the founder will derive all the benefits" (Victor Bérard, *L'Angleterre et l'Impérialisme,* cited in León Donnadieu, *Essai sur la Théorie de l'Equilibre,* Paris, 1900) and with which the United States identifies itself, is the new formula of the Doctrine, broader than previous formulas.

After seeing the United States join with other powers in Crete, Turkey, and China, and hearing Lord [Joseph] Chamberlain praise the excellencies of the Anglo-Saxon race, summoned to be "the dominant force in future history," and the advantages of imperialism, "of which an Englishman cannot speak without a glow of enthusiasm," one concludes that the words "America for the Americans" might be appropriately replaced by these others: "The world for the Anglo-Saxons."

THE THREE
MONROE DOCTRINES

Carlos Pereyra

Typical of the Latin-American reactions against the "imperialistic Monroeism" represented by Theodore Roosevelt's Corollary to the Monroe Doctrine and the subsequent interventions by the United States in the countries of Middle America is the following excerpt from a chapter by a Mexican publicist, Carlos Pereyra, in his *El Mito de Monroe* (1914). Pereyra served as a professor of history and sociology in the National University of Mexico and represented his country on diplomatic missions to Cuba, the United States, Belgium, and Holland. He was a prolific author, his works including *La Doctrina de Monroe* (1908), *El Crimen de Woodrow Wilson* (1917) *La Constitución de los Estados Unidos, Como Instrumento de Dominación* (1917?), and *Historia de América Española* in eight volumes (1920–1926). He died in 1942, in Spain.

There is not just one Monroe Doctrine. I know at least three, and perhaps there are others that I do not know. Three there are, in any case. . . .

Carlos Pereyra, *El Mito de Monroe* (Buenos Aires: Ediciones El Buho, 1959). First edition, 1914. Pp. 9, 12, 13, 30, 119. Translated by the editor.

The first Monroe Doctrine is the one which Secretary of State John Quincy Adams wrote and which, incorporated by Monroe in his presidential message of December 2, 1823, was immediately buried in complete oblivion, if not in actual words at least in its original meaning, and which from this viewpoint is known only as an antiquarian relic laboriously studied by a few investigators for the benefit of a small group of the curious-minded.

The second Monroe Doctrine is the one which has evolved, like something in popular legend, from Monroe's text into a kind of widespread dogma in glorification of the United States, taking form finally in the report submitted to President Grant by Secretary of State Fish on July 14, 1870, in the report of Secretary of State Bayard on January 20, 1887, and in the instructions of [Secretary of] State Olney to the Ambassador in London, Bayard, on June 20, 1895.

The third Monroe Doctrine is the one which, while based upon the declarations of these public men and their reckless falsifications of the original Monroe Doctrine, tries to represent the foreign policy of the United States as an idealized product of the original Doctrine. This last form of Monroeism, though being different from the preceding, is still not a falsification but rather an original conception by the creators and representatives of the imperialist movement: MacKinley [*sic*], Roosevelt, and Lodge; the representative of dollar diplomacy, Taft; and the representative of the tutelary, imperialist, financial, and biblical mission, Wilson.

To begin with, the Doctrine is not a doctrine. And then it is not Monroe's, as everyone knows.

The only value the declaration of 1823 associated with the name of the President of the United States can have is that of a historical fact, of an undeniable manifestation of force, but in fact it is nothing more than a chimera, an anachronism, and a supersitition.

The Monroe Doctrine has all the appearances and the reality of a taboo, that is to say, of a prohibition essentially magic with sanctions of the same kind.

From the viewpoint of international law there is not a single serious word in the Monroe Doctrine, and all the applications of it which have been made in diplomatic relations are what the Spaniards call *toreo alegre* (bull-baiting) or, better, a kind of trickery which came to be accepted in both theory and practice without serious question only because of the lack of important European interests involved in the processes of expansion.

. . . . .

The Monroe Doctrine forms part of the sentimental life of the United States and is associated, no less intimately and with the same ties, with the sentimental life of the other countries of America which enjoy either a nominal or an effective independence. We must study it, therefore, as one studies a belief, as we study, for example, the superstitions of a people in Polynesia. Is it not a question of a taboo, as we have said above? And a taboo, according to ethnology, is nothing but a prohibition of a religious and magical character to be enforced with a religious and magical sanction.

. . . . .

Some recent North American critics of the Monroe Doctrine say that it is an anachronism, an ancient relic which has fallen into disuse.

I believe that, on the contrary, the Monroe Doctrine is a vivid reality, a myth which serves as a wrapper concealing the actual fact, namely, the ambitions of a strong people who claim to exercise hegemony over a group of weak peoples, giving to their domination over them the hypocritical appearances of disinterest and benevolence.

In the past century of independence the American nations owe nothing to the United States in the way of protection nor promotion of their progress.

The great nations of the south have developed, and, above all, have lived by their own strength and by the influence of Europe. Those that are still in the process of formation have their eyes turned toward Europe in search of the materials of progress.

Mexico, for example, if it owes anything to the United States, owes the loss of a great part of its territory and the encouragement of barbarism which has bathed in blood the parts of its territory not conquered [by the United States]. . . .

I do not deny that some American countries, by exception and occasionally, owe some benefit to the Anglo-Americans, but it is a fact, acknowledged by their own writers, that the United States has not known how to develop a policy, even temporarily, toward the other countries of the continent. . . .

On what nation of the continent has the United States

not left the traces of some offense, contrary many times to
its own national interest?

. . . . .

Like everything that rests on faith, the defense of the
independence of the Ibero-American republics as the work
of the Monroe Doctrine or the phrases of Monroe is something which cannot be dismissed. He who does not believe
will ask in vain to be shown in all intellectual honesty just
what has been that defense of the American nations by the
United States. He who does believe will ask in turn to be
shown how the United States has not fulfilled nobly and
effectively the role of guardian of the integrity of the Americas. If it is asked on what occasions the United States has
weakened the action of Europe, the faithful will answer like
one following the light of the column of fire which guides
him in his way through the desert: "Such occasions have not
occurred—if we accept the anti-Monroe interpretation of
the case of the French intervention in Mexico—they have
not occurred because Mr. Monroe was standing guard. To
him, to his Doctrine, to his tradition all the republics of this
continent owe their beautiful independence." When an in-
terlocutor speaks with me in these terms, I change the subject and talk about the weather.

THE REAL
MONROE DOCTRINE

Elihu Root

The historical origins of the Monroe Doctrine were
traced and its meaning analyzed by former Secretary of
State Elihu Root (1845–1937) in an address which he
delivered as president of the American Society of
International Law at its eighth annual meeting in
Washington, D.C., on April 22, 1914. As President
McKinley's Secretary of War, Root made outstanding
contributions in developing policy for the administration
of Cuba and the new colonial possessions of the United
States. He served as Secretary of State under Theodore Roosevelt from 1905 to 1909 and was awarded
the Nobel Peace Prize in 1912 for his achievement in
establishing friendly relations with Latin America and
Japan.

The occasion for these declarations [by President Monroe
on December 2, 1823] is a familiar story—the revolt of the
Spanish provinces in America which Spain, unaided, was

Elihu Root, "The Real Monroe Doctrine," *American Journal of
International Law,* VIII (1914), 428–442. Reprinted by permission of
the publisher.

plainly unable to reduce to their former condition of dependence; the reaction against liberalism in Europe which followed the downfall of Napoleon and the restoration of the Bourbons to the throne of France; the formation of the Holy Alliance; the agreement of its members at the conferences of Aix-la-Chapelle, and Laybach, and Verona for the insurance of monarchy against revolution; the restoration of Ferdinand the Seventh to the throne of Spain by the armed power of France pursuant to this agreement; the purpose of the Alliance to follow the restoration of monarchy in Spain by the restoration of that monarchy's control over its colonies in the New World; the claims both of Russia and of Great Britain to rights of colonization on the Northwest coast; the proposals of Mr. Canning to Richard Rush for a joint declaration of principles by England and the United States adverse to the interference of any other European power in the contest between Spain and her former colonies; the serious question raised by this proposal as to the effect of a joint declaration upon the American policy of avoiding entangling alliances.

The form and phrasing of President Monroe's message were adapted to meet these conditions. The statements made were intended to carry specific information to the members of the Holy Alliance that an attempt by any of them to coerce the new states of South America would be not a simple expedition against weak and disunited colonies, but the much more difficult and expensive task of dealing with the formidable maritime power of the United States as well as the opposition of England, and they were intended to carry to Russia and incidentally to England the idea that rights to territory in the New World must thenceforth rest upon then existing titles, and that the United States would dispute any attempt to create rights to territory by future occupation.

It is undoubtedly true that the specific occasions for the declaration of Monroe no longer exist. The Holy Alliance long ago disappeared. The nations of Europe no longer contemplate the vindication of monarchical principles in the territory of the New World. France, the most active of the Allies, is herself a republic. No nation longer asserts the right of colonization in America. The general establishment of diplomatic relations between the powers of Europe and the American republics, if not already universal, became so when, pursuant to the formal assent of the powers, all the American republics were received into the Second Conference at The Hague and joined in the conventions there made, upon the footing of equal sovereignty, entitled to have their territory and independence respected under that law of nations which formerly existed for Europe alone.

The declaration, however, did more than deal with the specific occasion which called it forth. It was intended to declare a general principle for the future, and this is plain not merely from the generality of the terms used but from the discussions out of which they arose and from the understanding of the men who took part in the making and of their successors.

When Jefferson was consulted by President Monroe before the message was sent he replied:

> The question presented by the letters you have sent me is the most momentous which has ever been offered to my contemplation since that of independence. That made us a nation; this sets our compass and points the course which we are to steer through the ocean of time opening on us. And never could we embark upon it under circumstances more auspicious. Our first and fundamental maxim should be, never to entangle ourselves in the broils of Europe; our second, never to suffer Europe to intermeddle with cisatlantic affairs.

Three years later Daniel Webster declared that the Doctrine involved the honor of the country. He said in the House of Representatives:

> I look upon it as a part of its treasures of reputation; and, for one, I intend to guard it. . . . I will neither help to erase it or tear it out; nor shall it be, by any act of mine, blurred or blotted. It did honor to the sagacity of the government, and will not diminish that honor.

Mr. Cleveland said in his message of December 17, 1895:

> The Doctrine upon which we stand is strong and sound because its enforcement is important to our peace and safety as a nation, and is essential to the integrity of our free institutions and the tranquil maintenance of our distinctive form of government. It was

intended to apply to every stage of our national life and cannot become obsolete while our republic endures.

As the particular occasions which called it forth have slipped back into history, the declaration itself, instead of being handed over to the historian, has grown continually a more vital and insistent rule of conduct for each succeeding generation of Americans. Never for a moment have the responsible and instructed statesmen in charge of the foreign affairs of the United States failed to consider themselves bound to insist upon its policy. Never once has the public opinion of the people of the United States failed to support every just application of it as new occasion has arisen. Almost every President and Secretary of State has restated the Doctrine with vigor and emphasis in the discussion of the diplomatic affairs of his day. The governments of Europe have gradually come to realize that the existence of the policy which Monroe declared is a stubborn and continuing fact to be recognized in their controversies with American countries. We have seen Spain, France, England, Germany, with admirable good sense and good temper, explaining beforehand to the United States that they intended no permanent occupation of territory, in the controversy with Mexico forty years after the declaration, and in the controversy with Venezuela eighty years after. In 1903 the Duke of Devonshire declared "Great Britain accepts the Monroe Doctrine unreservedly." Mr. Hay coupled the Monroe Doctrine and the Golden Rule as cardinal guides of American diplomacy. Twice within very recent years the whole treaty-making power of the United States has given its formal approval to the policy by the reservations in the signature and in the ratification of the arbitration conventions of The Hague Conferences, expressed in these words by the Senate resolution agreeing to ratification of the convention of 1907:

Nothing contained in this convention shall be so construed as to require the United States of America to depart from its traditional policy of not intruding upon, interfering with, or entangling itself in the political questions of policy or internal administration of any foreign state, nor shall anything contained in the said convention be construed to imply a relinquishment by the United States of its traditional attitude towards purely American questions.

It seems fair to assume that a policy with such a history as this has some continuing and substantial reason underlying it; that it is not outworn or meaningless or a purely formal relic of the past, and it seems worth while to consider carefully what the Doctrine is and what it is not.

No one ever pretended that Mr. Monroe was declaring a rule of international law or that the Doctrine which he declared has become international law. It is a declaration of the United States that certain acts would be injurious to the peace and safety of the United States and that the United States would regard them as unfriendly.

. . . . .

The Doctrine is not international law but it rests upon the right of self-protection and that right is recognized by international law. The right is a necessary corollary of independent sovereignty. It is well understood that the exercise of the right of self-protection may and frequently does extend in its effect beyond the limits of the territorial jurisdiction of the state exercising it. The strongest example probably would be the mobilization of an army by another power immediately across the frontier. Every act done by the other power may be within its own territory. Yet the country threatened by the state of facts is justified in protecting itself by immediate war. The most common exercise of the right of self-protection outside of a state's own territory and in time of peace is the interposition of objection to the occupation of territory, of points of strategic military or maritime advantage, or to indirect accomplishment of this effect by dynastic arrangement. For example, the objection of England in 1911 to the occupation of a naval station by Germany on the Atlantic coast of Morocco; the objection of the European powers generally to the vast force of Russia extending its territory to the Mediterranean; the revision of the Treaty of San Stefano by the Treaty of Berlin; the establishment of buffer states; the objection to the succession of a German prince to the throne of Spain; the many forms of the eastern question; the centuries of struggle to preserve the balance of power in Europe; all depend upon the very same principle which underlies the Monroe Doctrine; that is to say, upon the right of every sovereign state to protect itself by preventing a condition of affairs in which it will be too late to protect itself. Of course each state must judge for itself when a threatened act will create such a situation. If any state objects to a threatened act and the reasonableness of its objection is not assented to, the efficacy of the objection will depend upon the power behind it.

It is doubtless true that in the adherence of the American people to the original declaration there was a great element of sentiment and sympathy for the people of South America who were struggling for freedom, and it has been a source of great satisfaction to the United States that the course which it took in 1823 concurrently with the action of Great Britain played so great a part in assuring the right of self-government to the countries of South America. Yet it is to be observed that in reference to the South American governments, as in all other respects, the international right upon which the declaration expressly rests is not sentiment or sympathy or a claim to dictate what kind of government any other country shall have, but the safety of the United States. It is because the new governments cannot be overthrown by the allied powers "without endangering our peace and happiness" that "the United States cannot behold such interposition in any form with indifference."

We frequently see statements that the Doctrine has been changed or enlarged; that there is a new or different Doctrine since Monroe's time. They are mistaken. There has been no change. One apparent extension of the statement of Monroe was made by President Polk in his messages of 1845 and 1848, when he included the acquisition of territory by a European power through cession as dangerous to the safety of the United States. It was really but stating a corollary to the Doctrine of 1823 and asserting the same right of self-protection against the other American states as well as against Europe.

This corollary has been so long and uniformly agreed to by the government and the people of the United States that it may fairly be regarded as being now a part of the Doctrine.

But, all assertions to the contrary notwithstanding, there

has been no other change or enlargement of the Monroe Doctrine since it was first promulgated. It must be remembered that not everything said or written by Secretaries of State or even by Presidents constitutes a national policy or can enlarge or modify or diminish a national policy.

It is the substance of the thing to which the nation holds and that is and always has been that the safety of the United States demands that American territory shall remain American.

The Monroe Doctrine does not assert or imply or involve any right on the part of the United States to impair or control the independent sovereignty of any American state. In the lives of nations, as of individuals, there are many rights unquestioned and universally conceded. The assertion of any particular right must be considered, not as excluding all others but as coincident with all others which are not inconsistent. The fundamental principle of international law is the principle of independent sovereignty. Upon that all other rules of international law rest. That is the chief and necessary protection of the weak against the power of the strong. Observance of that is the necessary condition to the peace and order of the civilized world. By the declaration of that principle the common judgment of civilization awards to the smallest and weakest state the liberty to control its own affairs without interference from any other power, however great.

The Monroe Doctrine does not infringe upon that right. It asserts the right. The declaration of Monroe was that the rights and interests of the United States were involved in maintaining a condition, and the condition to be maintained was the independence of all the American countries. It is "the free and independent condition which they have assumed and maintained" which is declared to render them not subject to future colonization. It is "the governments who have declared their independence and maintained it and whose independence we have on great consideration and on just principles acknowledged" that are not to be interfered with. When Mr. Canning's proposals for a joint declaration were under consideration by the Cabinet in the month before the famous message was sent, John Quincy Adams, who played the major part in forming the policy, declared the basis of it in these words:

Considering the South Americans as independent nations, they themselves and no other nation had the right to dispose of their condition. We have no right to dispose of them either alone or in conjunction with other nations. Neither have any other nations the right of disposing of them without their consent.

In the most critical and momentous application of the Doctrine Mr. Seward wrote to the French Minister:

France need not for a moment delay her promised withdrawal of military forces from Mexico and her putting the principle of non-intervention into full and complete practice in regard to Mexico through any apprehension that the United States will prove unfaithful to the principles and policy in that respect which on their behalf it has been my duty to maintain in this now very lengthened correspondence. The practice of this government from its beginning is a guarantee to all nations of the respect of the American people for the free sovereignty of the people in every other state. We received the instruction from Washington. We applied it sternly in our early intercourse even with France. The same principle and practice have been uniformly inculcated by all our statesmen, interpreted by all our jurists, maintained by all our Congresses, and acquiesced in without practical dissent on all occasions by the American people. It is in reality the chief element of foreign intercourse in our history.

In his message to Congress of December 3, 1906, President Roosevelt said:

In many parts of South America there has been much misunderstanding of the attitude and purposes of the United States toward the other American republics. An idea had become prevalent that our assertion of the Monroe Doctrine implied or carried with it an assumption of superiority and of a right to exercise some kind of protectorate over the countries to whose territory that Doctrine applies. Nothing could be farther from the truth.

He quoted the words of the Secretary of State then in office [Elihu Root] to the recent Pan-American Conference at Rio de Janeiro:

We deem the independence and equal rights of the smallest and weakest member of the family of nations entitled to as much respect as those of the greatest empire and we deem the observance of that respect the chief guaranty of the weak against the oppression of the strong. We neither claim nor desire any rights or privileges or powers that we do not freely concede to every American republic.

And the President then proceeded to say of these statements:

They have my hearty approval, as I am sure they will have yours, and I cannot be wrong in the conviction that they correctly represent the sentiments of the whole American people. I cannot better characterize the true attitude of the United States in its assertion of the Monroe Doctrine than in the words of the distinguished former Minister of Foreign Affairs of Argentina, Doctor Drago . . . "the traditional policy of the United States without accentuating superiority or seeking preponderance condemned the oppression of the nations of this part of the world and the control of their destinies by the great powers of Europe."

Curiously enough, many incidents and consequences of that independent condition itself which the United States asserted in the Monroe Doctrine have been regarded in some quarters as infringements upon independence resulting from the Monroe Doctrine. Just as the personal rights of each individual free citizen in the state are limited by the equal rights of every other free individual in the same state, so the sovereign rights of each independent state are limited by the equal sovereign rights of every other independent state. These limitations are not impairments of independent sovereignty. They are the necessary conditions to the existence of independent sovereignty. If the Monroe Doctrine had never been declared or thought of, the sovereign rights of each American republic would have been limited by the equal sovereign rights of every other American republic, including the United States. The United States would have had a right to demand from every other American state observance of treaty obligations and of the rules of international law. It would have had the right to insist upon due protection for the lives and property of its citizens within the territory of every other American state, and upon the treatment of its citizens in that territory according to the rules of international law. The United States would have had the right as against every other American state to object to acts which the United States might deem injurious to its peace and safety just as it had the right to object to such acts as against any European power and just as all European and American powers have the right to object to such acts as against each other. All these rights which the United States would have had as against other American states it has now. They are not in the slightest degree affected by the Monroe Doctrine. They exist now just as they would have existed if there had been no Monroe Doctrine. They are neither greater nor less because of that Doctrine. They are not rights of superiority, they are rights of equality. They are the rights which all equal independent states have as against each other. And they cover the whole range of peace and war.

It happens, however, that the United States is very much bigger and more powerful than most of the other American republics. And when a very great and powerful state makes demands upon a very small and weak state it is difficult to avoid a feeling that there is an assumption of superior authority involved in the assertion of superior power, even though the demand be based solely upon the right of equal against equal. An examination of the various controversies which the United States has had with other American powers will disclose the fact that in every case the rights asserted were rights not of superiority but of equality. Of course it cannot be claimed that great and powerful states shall forego their just rights against smaller and less powerful states. The responsibilities of sovereignty attach to the weak as well as to the strong, and a claim to exemption from those responsibilities would imply not equality but inferiority. The most that can be said concerning a question between a powerful state and a weak one is that the great state ought to be especially considerate and gentle in the assertion and maintenance of its position; ought always to base its acts not upon a superiority of force, but upon reason and law; and ought to assert no rights against a small state because of its weakness which it would not assert against a great state notwithstanding its power. But in all this the Monroe Doctrine is not concerned at all.

The scope of the Doctrine is strictly limited. It concerns itself only with the occupation of territory in the New World to the subversion or exclusion of a pre-existing American government. It has not otherwise any relation to the affairs of either American or European states. In good conduct or bad, observance of rights or violations of them, agreement or controversy, injury or reprisal, coercion or war, the United States finds no warrant in the Monroe Doctrine for interference. So Secretary Cass wrote, in 1858:

> With respect to the causes of war between Spain and Mexico, the United States have no concern, and do not undertake to judge them. Nor do they claim to interpose in any hostilities which may take place. Their policy of observation and interference is limited to the permanent subjugation of any portion of the territory of Mexico, or of any other American state, to any European power whatever.

So Mr. Seward wrote, in 1861, concerning the allied operation against Mexico:

> As the undersigned has heretofore had the honor to inform each of the plenipotentiaries now addressed, the President does not feel at liberty to question, and does not question, that the sovereigns represented have undoubted right to decide for themselves the fact whether they have sustained grievances, and to resort to war against Mexico for the redress thereof, and have a right also to levy the war severally or jointly.

So when Germany, Great Britain, and Italy united to compel by naval force a response to their demands on the part of Venezuela and the German government advised the United States that it proposed to take coercive measures to enforce its claims for damages and for money against Venezuela, adding, "We declare especially that under no circumstances do we consider in our proceedings the acquisition or permanent occupation of Venezuelan territory," Mr. Hay replied that the government of the United States, although it

> regretted that European powers should use force against Central and South American countries, could not object to their taking steps to obtain redress for injuries suffered by their subjects, provided that no acquisition of territory was contemplated.

Quite independently of the Monroe Doctrine, however, there is a rule of conduct among nations under which each nation is deemed bound to render the good offices of friendship to the others when they are in trouble. The rule has been crystallized in the provisions of The Hague Convention for the Pacific Settlement of International Disputes. Under the head of "The Maintenance of General Peace" in that Convention substantially all the powers of the world have agreed:

> With a view to obviating as far as possible recourse to force in the relations between states, the contracting powers agree to use their best efforts to ensure the pacific settlement of international differences.
>
> In case of serious disagreement or dispute, before an appeal to arms, the contracting powers agree to have recourse, as far as circumstances allow, to the good offices or mediation of one or more friendly powers.
>
> Independently of this recourse, the contracting powers deem it expedient and desirable that one or more powers, strangers to the dispute, should, on their own initiative and as far as circumstances may allow, offer their good offices or mediation to the states at variance. . . . The exercise of this right can never be regarded by either of the parties in dispute as an unfriendly act.
>
> The part of the mediator consists in reconciling the opposing claims and appeasing the feelings of resentment which may have arisen between the states at variance.

The United States has frequently performed this duty in controversies between American republics among themselves and between American republics and European states. So in the controversy last referred to, the United States used its good offices to bring about a series of arbitrations which superseded the resort to force determined upon by the allied powers against Venezuela. She did this upon the request of Venezuela. She did it in the performance of no duty and the exercise of no right whatever except the duty and the right of friendship between equal sovereign states. The Monroe Doctrine has nothing whatever to do with acts of this description; yet many times censorious critics, unfamiliar with the facts and uninstructed in the customs and rules of action of the international world, have accused the United States in such cases of playing the role of school master, of assuming the superiority of guardianship, of aiming at a protectorate.

As the Monroe Doctrine neither asserts nor involves any right of control by the United States over any American nation, it imposes upon the United States no duty towards European powers to exercise such a control. It does not call upon the United States to collect debts or coerce conduct or redress wrongs or revenge injuries. If matters ever came to a point where in any American country the United States intervenes by force to prevent or end an occupation of territory to the subversion or exclusion of an American government, doubtless new rights and obligations will arise as a result of the acts done in the course of the intervention. Unless such a situation shall have arisen there can be no duty on the part of the United States beyond the exercise of good offices as between equal and independent nations.

There are indeed special reasons why the United States should perform that duty of equal friendship to the full limit of international custom and international ethics as declared in The Hague Convention, whenever occasion arises in controversy between American and European powers. There is a motive for that in the special sympathy and friendship for the gradually developing republics of the south which the American people have always felt since the days of Monroe and John Quincy Adams and Richard Rush and Henry Clay. There is a motive in the strong desire of our government that no controversy between a European and an American state shall ever come to the point where the United States may be obliged to assert by force the rule of national safety declared by Monroe. And there is a motive in the proper desire of the United States that no friendly nation of Europe or America shall be injured or hindered in the prosecution of its rights in any way or to any extent that can possibly be avoided because that nation respects the rule of safety which Mr. Monroe declared and we maintain. None of these reasons for the exercise of the good offices of equality justifies nor do all of them together justify the United States in infringing upon the independence or ignoring the equal rights of the smallest American state.

Nor has the United States ever in any instance during the period of almost a century which has elapsed made the Monroe Doctrine, or the motives which lead us to support it, the ground or excuse for overstepping the limits which the rights of equal sovereignty set between equal sovereign states.

Since the Monroe Doctrine is a declaration based upon this nation's right of self-protection, it cannot be transmuted into a joint or common declaration by American states or any number of them. If Chile or Argentina or Brazil were to contribute the weight of her influence toward a similar end, the right upon which that nation would rest its declaration would be its own safety, not the safety of the United States. Chile would declare what was necessary for the safety of Chile. Argentina would declare what was necessary for the safety of Argentina. Brazil, what was necessary for the safety of Brazil. Each nation would act for itself and in its own right and it would be impossible to go beyond that except by more or less offensive and defensive alliances. Of course such alliances are not to be considered.

. . . . .

The danger to be apprehended from the immediate proximity of hostile forces was not the sole consideration leading to the declaration. The need to separate the influences determining the development and relation of states in the New World from the influences operating in Europe played an even greater part. The familiar paragraphs of Washington's Farewell Address upon this subject were not rhetoric. They were intensely practical rules of conduct for the future guidance of the country.

Europe has a set of primary interests, which to us have none, or a very remote relation. Hence, she must be engaged in frequent controversies, the causes of which are essentially foreign to our concerns. Hence, therefore, it must be unwise in us to implicate ourselves, by artificial ties, in the ordinary vicissitudes of her politics, or the ordinary combinations and collisions of her friendships or enmities. Our detached and distant situation invites and enables us to pursue a different course.

It was the same instinct which led Jefferson, in the letter to Monroe already quoted, to say:

Our first and fundamental maxim should be, never to entangle ourselves in the broils of Europe; our second, never to suffer Europe to intermeddle with cisatlantic affairs.

The concurrence of Washington and Hamilton and Jefferson in the declaration of this principle of action entitles it to great respect. They recalled the long period during which every war waged in Europe between European powers and arising from European causes of quarrel was waged also in the New World. English and French and Spanish and Dutch killed and harried each other in America, not because of quarrels between the settlers in America but because of quarrels between the European powers having dominion over them. Separation of influences as absolute and complete as possible was the remedy which the wisest of Americans agreed upon. It was one of the primary purposes of Monroe's declaration to insist upon this separation, and to accomplish it he drew the line at the water's edge. The problem of national protection in the distant future is one not to be solved by the first impressions of the casual observer, but only by profound study of the forces which, in the long life of nations, work out results. In this case the results of such a study by the best men of the formative period of the United States are supported by the instincts of the American democracy holding steadily in one direction for almost a century. The problem has not changed essentially. If the declaration of Monroe was right when the message was sent, it is right now. South America is no more distant today than it was then. The tremendous armaments and international jealousies of Europe afford little assurance to those who think we may now abandon the separatist policy of Washington. That South American states have become too strong for colonization or occupation is cause for satisfaction. That Euope has no purpose or wish to colonize American territory is most gratifying. These facts may make it improbable that it will be necessary to apply the Monroe Doctrine in the southern parts of South America; but they furnish no reason whatever for retracting or denying or abandoning a declaration of public policy, just and reasonable when it was made, and which, if occasion for its application shall arise in the future, will still be just and reasonable.

A false conception of what the Monroe Doctrine is, of what it demands and what it justifies, of its scope and of its limits, has invaded the public press and affected public opinion within the past few years. Grandiose schemes of national expansion invoke the Monroe Doctrine. Interested motives to compel Central or South American countries to do or refrain from doing something by which individual Americans may profit invoke the Monroe Doctrine. Clamors for national glory from minds too shallow to grasp at the same time a sense of national duty invoke the Monroe Doctrine. The intolerance which demands that control over the conduct and the opinions of other peoples which is the essence of tyranny invokes the Monroe Doctrine. Thoughtless people who see no difference between lawful right and physical power assume that the Monroe Doctrine is a warrant for interference in the internal affairs of all weaker nations in the New World. Against this supposititious doctrine, many protests both in the United States and in South America have been made, and justly made. To the real Monroe Doctrine these protests have no application.

NEED FOR A
LATIN-AMERICAN UNION

José Ingenieros

The imperialism of the United States stimulated a re-
vival of the movement for Latin-American union as
opposed to the Pan American Union, which included
the United States. An Argentine sociologist, José Ingenieros (1877–1925), gave eloquent expression to this
movement of protest in an address honoring José Vasconcelos and delivered in Buenos Aires, Argentina, in
1922. Ingenieros, author of twenty-three volumes on
sociology, psychology, philosophy, medicine, and crim-
inology, exerted great influence in all these fields, as
well as in the area of political action, through his zeal
for radical reform. By the time of the following address
he had considerably moderated his earlier Marxist
orthodoxy.

We are not, we do not wish longer to be, we cannot continue to be Pan-Americanists. The famous Monroe Doctrine,
which has been made to appear for a century as the guaranty of our political independence against the danger of

José Ingenieros, "Por La Unión Latino Americana," *Nosotros*,
Buenos Aires, XVI (October 1922), [145]–158. Translated by the
editor.

European conquests, has revealed itself gradually to be a reservation of the right of North America to protect us and intervene in our affairs. The powerful neighbor and officious friend has developed the system of capitalist production to the highest degree and attained in the last war the hegemony of the world; with its economic power the appetite of its privileged caste has grown, tightening its control more and more in an imperialistic sense to convert the government into an instrument of the trusts without any other principles than to capture the sources of wealth and to gamble with human labor which is already enslaved under the iron rule of a banking aristocracy without pride of nation and without morals. In the governing classes of that great nation has meanwhile sprung up the aspiration for expansion and conquest to such a degree that the classic "America for the Americans" means nothing but "America—our Latin America—for the North Americans."

. . . The danger from the United States arises not from its inferiority but from its superiority; it is frightening because it is great, rich, and enterprising. We need to know if there is any possibility of counterbalancing its power in such a way as to safeguard our political independence and the sovereignty of our nations.

The hour is grave. The moment has come to decide if we ought to give a decisive "no" to Pan-Americanism and the Monroe Doctrine which as they have lost their original ambiguity appear now as instruments of deceit wielded by the imperialistic party which serves the interests of capitalism in the government.

If during the past century the Monroe Doctrine could be regarded as a guaranty of the "principle of nationalities" against the "right of intervention," today we see that that Doctrine, as currently interpreted, expresses the "right of intervention" by the United States against the "principle of nationalities" for the Latin Americans. From a hypothetical guaranty it has been converted into an effective danger.

We call its past guaranty only hypothetical; the facts prove it. Did the North Americans invoke the Monroe Doctrine in 1833, when England occupied the Malvinas [Falkland] Islands belonging to Argentina? Did they impose it in 1838 when the French squadron bombarded the castle of San Juan de Ulua? Did they resort to it in the following years when Admiral Leblanc blockaded the harbors of the Río de la Plata? And in 1861 when Spain conquered Santo Domingo? And in 1864 when Napoleon III imposed Emperor Maximilian of Austria upon Mexico? And in 1866 when Spain blockaded the ports of the Pacific? And 100 times more when on the pretext of collecting debts and protecting their subjects the European nations employed force and violence against our republics, as in the case of Venezuela?

That equivocal Doctrine, which has never been used to oppose European interventions, has finally taken on the function only of assuring to the North Americans a monopoly of interventions. Represented as the key which unlocked our independence, it has become the picklock of our future conquest; the skillful keeper of the keys pretended to take care of us for 100 years the best he could, though not for us but rather only for himself.

All this suggests to us the recent North American imperialist policy which has followed an alarming course for all Latin America. From the war with Spain it acquired Puerto Rico and imposed upon the independence of Cuba the annoying conditions of the shameful Platt Amendment. It did not wait long to amputate from Colombia the isthmus which would permit it to unite through Panama its Atlantic and Pacific coasts. It intervened then in Nicaragua in order to assure itself a possible route for another interoceanic canal. It threatened the sovereignty of Mexico with its unhappy venture at Veracruz. It possessed itself militarily of Haiti on childish pretexts. A little later it carried out the shameful occupation of Santo Domingo alleging the usual pretext of pacifying the country and managing its finances.

From that moment the madness of the imperialist party appeared to lose all restraint. The North American meddling in the politics of Mexico, Cuba, and Central America was unmasked. It seeks to exercise the right of intervention and applies it in fact, sometimes corrupting politicians with loans of money and at other times wronging the people with the shamelessness of its military expeditions.

Formerly and even today it is obstructing and dissolving the Central American Federation, knowing that all morsels can easily be devoured if they are divided into small mouthfuls. Formerly and even today it refuses to recognize the constitutional government of Mexico unless that government will sign treaties which include privileges for foreign capitalism which are hostile to the national interest. Formerly and even today it inflicts on Cuba the new indignity of imposing General Crowder as tutelary interventor.

But I read on many faces the objection: Panama is the natural limit of its expansion, and there capitalist imperialism will stop. Many truly believed this until a few years ago; we must admit it, although this sentiment of collective self-importance may not be very honorable for us. The most distant nations—Brazil, Uruguay, Argentina, and Chile— believed themselves protected from the claws of the eagle, trusting that the torrid zone would set a limit to its flight.

Some, finally, have seen that we were deceived. We know now that the voracious tentacles extend down both the Pacific and the Atlantic with the object of ensuring direct or indirect financial control over several of the southern nations. We know also—though it is a diplomatic secret—of vague negotiations concerning the Guianas. We know that some governments—which we do not name in order not to excite their susceptibilities—live under a guardianship in fact very similar to the ignominy sanctioned in law by the Platt Amendment. We know that certain recent loans contain clauses which provide for a financial controller and some form of intervention. And finally we know that for several years North American penetration has made itself felt with growing intensity in all the political, economic, and social machinery of South America.

Do we still doubt? Do we continue to believe naively that the imperialist ambition will stop at Panama? We should be blind if we did not note that the countries to the south are in the first phase of conquest, just as formerly occurred in the countries to the north which are now in the grip of the second phase.

. . . . .

. . . The danger does not begin with annexation as in Puerto Rico, nor with intervention as in Cuba, nor with a military expedition as in Mexico, nor with a protectorate as in Nicaragua, nor with a territorial seizure as in Colombia, nor with armed occupation as in Haiti, nor with purchase as in the Guianas. The danger, in its first phase, begins with the progressive mortgaging of national independence by means of loans which are self-perpetuating and self-augmenting under conditions each time more destructive of the sovereignty of the recipients. Years ago the Cuban apostle José Martí gave a warning which has been repeated with anguish by the eminent Enrique José Varona: We must be on our guard lest the cooperation of powerful friends be converted into a guardianship which is only a bridge to slavery.

Did not Wilson in an effort to win our sympathies say during the war that the right of small nations would be respected and that all peoples would be free to give themselves the government which seemed best to them? What became of his principles? How has his own country applied them? In Cuba by intervening in its politics? In Mexico by refusing to recognize the government which the Mexicans consider best? In Santo Domingo by replacing their own government with commissioned soldiers and by offering to withdraw from the island only after imposing unjust treaties? And what is to become of our national independence—that of all of us—if each new loan contains clauses which augment the financial and political control of the lender?

. . . . .

We believe that our nations are confronted with an iron dilemma: either to deliver ourselves submissively to the Pan American Union (America for the North Americans) or to unite in defending our independence and establishing the bases of a Latin American Union (Latin America for the Latin Americans). We know that this second task is enormous and difficult since already there are great interests opposing it in the form of powerful financial syndicates. But to become discouraged beforehand by the magnitude of the task is the same as surrendering; he is already conquered who considers himself conquered. To trust that distance will be a natural defense is only to transfer the danger to a place a little less near and to accept the cynical conclusion: after me the deluge! To suppose that greater political importance will furnish immunity for certain nations is to forget that Mexico has, by reason of its population and natural wealth, a pre-eminent position in Latin America, without which it might not have attracted imperialist capitalism. Who can guaranty that wheat and meat, petroleum and sugar, tobacco and coffee may not become natural enemies of our independence in the future in such proportion as our own abundance of them determines?

Who monopolizes and controls world markets? During the Great War who acquired the bonds of the great industrial, railway, and commercial corporations which European capital had established in Latin America? Who is the only lender to whom governments protest whenever their financial and administrative improvidence plunges them into crisis? By these means which affect us all, some more and some less, national sovereignty is being diminished and at the same time control and the right of intervention by the North Americans are being fixed upon us. It will not operate in the same way for all, for it is more difficult to oppress the great and the remote; but it will come later or under other forms: Cuba was not annexed with Puerto Rico nor was Mexico intervened as was Santo Domingo. What is certain, we firmly believe, is that it will come to all of us if we do not mobilize certain moral forces which will enable us to resist.

. . . . .

Moral forces must be invoked as an impelling inner drive among the Latin-American peoples which will serve as a basis for a future political and economic confederation capable of resisting jointly the operations of any foreign imperialism. The resistance which today no isolated nation can offer by itself will be possible if all are confederated.

The old plan, essentially political, of directly confederating governments appears at present to be unattainable, since the majority of them are subordinated to the control of North Americans who are their creditors. We must direct ourselves first to the people and create in them a new national conscience, broadening the concept and the feeling of the nation, making it continental in scope, since as the municipality broadens into the province and the province into the political state so naturally it must broaden into a confederation of peoples in which each one will be able to emphasize and develop its own characteristics motivated by a common cooperation and solidarity.

. . . . .

SHOULD WE ABANDON THE MONROE DOCTRINE?

Hiram Bingham

Hiram Bingham (1875–1956), famed as the discoverer of the lost city of the Incas, Machu Picchu, in 1911, became one of the most articulate United States critics of the Monroe Doctrine, which he condemned as "an obsolete shibboleth." As a professor at Yale University until 1924, he centered his academic interest around South America and wrote many books about that area and the relation of the United States to it, including *The Monroe Doctrine, An Obsolete Shibboleth* (1913) and *The Future of the Monroe Doctrine* (1920). He was elected Governor of Connecticut in 1924. Later that same year he was elected a Senator and represented Connecticut in the United States Senate from 1924 to 1933. While Senator, Bingham announced that he had changed his views as to the Monroe Doctrine because, as he explained to the Senate on January 8, 1927, he became convinced by the German threat in World War I that the United States must retain the

Hiram Bingham, "Should We Abandon the Monroe Doctrine?" *Journal of Race Development*, Worcester, Mass., IV (January 1914), 334–358.

Doctrine, "at least so far as the Caribbean Sea and the countries bordering on it were concerned."

"The Monroe Doctrine, or the doctrine of the dual political organization of the nations of the earth, is a barbaric stumbling-block in the way of enlightened international policy." So wrote the late William Graham Sumner, in an essay on "Earth Hunger," in 1897.

. . . . .

During the past few months the number of people who have come to take an unfriendly attitude toward the Monroe Doctrine has very greatly increased. True, this national shibboleth is still a plank in the platforms of our great national parties. In many quarters it is still a rallying cry. A great chain of newspapers, extending from San Francisco to Boston, edited by the most highly paid editorial writer of the day, constantly refers to the Monroe Doctrine as something sacred and precious, like the Declaration of Independence. Other powerful newspapers, less popular in their appeal, but no less powerful in their influence, still resent any attack on what is considered by them the most essential feature of our foreign policy. And they continue to uphold the Monroe Doctrine, while at the same time they try to explain away its disagreeable features.

A recent editorial in a journal devoted to the interests of the army and navy, in vigorously denouncing the present attacks being made on the Monroe Doctrine, and calling loudly on patriotic Americans to see to it that no academic sentimentalists were allowed to weaken our national defenses, declared that without the Monroe Doctrine we could not hold the Panama Canal!

It would have been just as logical to say that without the Monroe Doctrine we could not hold Hawaii, or Key West, or Boston harbor. The Panama Canal is one of the possessions of the United States. Its defense is a national right and a national duty. In defending the Panama Canal as in defending Key West or Boston harbor, we have back of us the most universally accepted principles of international law. In upholding the Monroe Doctrine, on the other hand, we are merely upholding what has been believed for many years to be a useful foreign policy, but one that has no standing in international law, and is, in fact, neither law nor doctrine but merely a declaration of policy having to do with our relations with foreign nations.

Consequently, in considering the question as to whether we should abandon the Monroe Doctrine or not, we must first clear our minds of any idea that the maintenance or abandonment of this policy is in any way synonymous with the maintenance or abandonment of our national defenses, be they in Hawaii, Boston harbor, or the Panama Canal. Of course, it is perfectly true that to maintain a vigorous foreign policy and one that is at all unpopular means the maintenance of an efficient army and navy. But without any vigorous foreign policy we should, at the same time, need an army and a navy, and both ought to be efficient for the same reason that every city needs an efficient police force.

In considering the advisability of abandoning the Monroe Doctrine, let us attempt to get clearly in mind exactly what is meant by the Monroe Doctrine. We shall find that at different periods of our history, it has meant very different things. When it was promulgated by President Monroe in 1823, it meant that we were afraid that the rising wave of monarchy and despotism in Europe might overwhelm the struggling republics in the New World. We were, in a sense, in the position of the big brother on the edge of the swimming pool, who sees his little brothers swimming under water and about to come to the surface, and who also sees a couple of bullies getting ready to duck them before they can get their breath. As a matter of fact, this was the only republic, at that time, that had come to the surface, scrambled on to the bank, and shown itself able to stand on its own legs. The little fellows in Spanish America were swimming hard, but they had not got their heads above water. We believed it to be for our interests to see that they had a square deal and were not interfered with as they came to the surface. We promulgated a high-minded, unselfish policy, without a thought of gaining prestige or power in Latin America. We bravely warned the nations of the continent of Europe not to attempt to inflict their system of government on any land in the Western Hemisphere where a democratic or republican form of government had established itself.

From such a high-minded and altruistic position as this, it is a far cry to the connotation which goes with the Monroe Doctrine in the minds of many American citizens of to-day. . . . In 1823, this declaration of foreign policy made a profound impression on Europe, and won us the gratitude and the eulogies of the Latin-American republics. At the present time, there is no question that the Monroe Doctrine is a cause of world-wide irritation and is almost universally hated throughout Latin America. In the words of a careful student of Pan-American affairs who has lived many years in various parts of Spanish America, "the two principal results of the Monroe Doctrine are: intense hatred of the United States on the part of powerful and self-respecting South American nations, able and willing to meet their responsibilities to the countries to whom they are under obligations; and an attempt at evasion of these responsibilities by other Latin-American countries, who, while using the Doctrine where they think they can for such a purpose, equally hate the originators of it."

. . . . .

Before deciding whether we ought to abandon the Monroe Doctrine and considering what ought to be our policy for the future, let us review a few of the more striking features of our foreign policy since 1823.

For twenty years after the promulgation of the Monroe Doctrine, we were regarded with extraordinary friendliness throughout Spanish America. Our willingness to recognize the independence of the newly-fledged republics, our willingness to protect them from European aggression, and our generous non-interference with them in the time of their greatest weakness, earned us their gratitude. But in 1846 came the war with Mexico, one of those independent republics that we were going to protect. We had stated in the original Monroe Doctrine that it was the true policy of the United States to leave the new governments of Spanish America to themselves, in the hope that other powers would pursue the same course. And yet, we did not hesitate, at the conclusion of the war with Mexico, to take away from her nearly one half her area. It did not help matters that a year or two later gold was discovered in California. It did not increase our popularity in Spanish America when it appeared that we were getting enormously wealthy out of the gold and silver mines in California and Nevada, which we had so recently taken by force from Mexico, even though we had paid $15,000,000 for what we took. It may be replied that it was far better for California and Nevada that we should have taken them, and that we could afford to stand the unpopularity that this engendered in South America. Granting for the sake of argument that this is true, why not admit frankly that when we took California and Nevada, we went contrary to the principles laid down by President Monroe in his famous message of 1823.

In 1898, we went to war with Spain, and eventually took away all her American possessions. We believed ourselves justified in so doing. I hold no brief against the justification of that war. It was undoubtedly a good thing for Spain. Many Spaniards will admit this today. Their country has been stronger and their economic condition has improved since they lost their foreign possessions. But President Monroe had said that "With the existing colonies or dependencies of any European power, we have not interfered and shall not interfere." Is it not perfectly evident that in 1898 we regarded the Monroe Doctrine as outgrown, and said to ourselves that we could afford to disregard one of the most positive sentences in the original declaration of President Monroe? Why should we still feel that there is something so sacred in this national shibboleth of ours that, although we have repeatedly gone contrary to it when it suited us to do so, we must still cling to it as a precious thing, without which our own independence would be in danger of being lost?

In 1906, Secretary Root made his well-known tour of South America. It has been said that this tour was made necessary owing to the fear of the United States aroused throughout South America by some of President Roosevelt's messages to Congress, in which he took pains to reassert the Monroe Doctrine, and in which he accepted, quite logically, the very great responsibilities which the maintenance of a policy of "America for the Americans" entailed upon us. He had said in 1905:

When we announce a policy, such as the Monroe Doctrine, we thereby commit ourselves to the consequences of the policy, and those consequences from time to time alter. It is out of the question to claim a right and then to shirk the responsibility for its exercise. Not only we, but all American republics who are benefited by the existence of the Doctrine, must recognize the obligations each nation is under as regards foreign peoples no less than its duty to insist upon its own rights.

After the opening of the third session of the Fifty-Eighth Congress, Mr. Roosevelt had said:

Any country whose people conduct themselves well can count upon our hearty friendship. If a nation shows that it knows how to act with reasonable efficiency and decency in social and political matters, if it keeps order and pays its obligations, it need fear no interference from the United States. Chronic wrongdoing, or an impotence which results in a general loosening of the ties of civilized society, may in America, as elsewhere, ultimately require intervention by some civilized nation, and in the Western Hemisphere, the adherence of the United States to the Monroe Doctrine may force the United States, however reluctantly, in flagrant cases of such wrongdoing or impotence, to the exercise of an international police power.

These official utterances had greatly alarmed and annoyed the South American republics, and it was no small part of Secretary Root's visit to quiet their fears and assure them of the pacific quality of our intentions. So well did Mr. Root do this, so ably had he prepared himself by the study of South American history, so favorable an impression did he make by his dignified and courteous bearing, and so profound a conviction did his words convey, coming as they did from the actual head of our department of foreign affairs, that great good was accomplished, and an era of friendship and good-will was ushered in.

. . . . .

We do desire to influence for good the Western Hemisphere. We are beginning to realize that there are several states in South America that are no longer infant republics. They have grown up. To return to our former metaphor—the little swimmers have got their heads well out of water, and have climbed out and are safely standing on their own legs. They naturally resent any implied assertion on our part that we will protect them from Europe.

If the Monroe Doctrine implies this we-will-protect-you-from-Europe attitude, if it is disagreeable and irritating to those whose friendship is most worth having in the Western Hemisphere, if, as a matter of fact, we have deliberately broken the Monroe Doctrine whenever it suited us to do so, why should we cling to it so tenderly and so tenaciously any longer? What possible good can it do us? We apparently have a great deal to lose by maintaining it. What have we to gain by pretending to stick to it?

The chief arguments in favor of retaining the Monroe Doctrine appear to be three:

The first is, that the good old Doctrine is ninety years of age; it has survived and flourished nearly a century, and there *must* be *something* in it to have given it such a long life! To such an argument as this, it is only necessary to reply that the same notion was used with even more telling effect against Copernicus, when he declared that the world revolved on its axis. Furthermore, it sounds suspiciously like the defense that we made of slavery in the middle of the nineteenth century. It is an argument that need not be treated seriously.

In the second place, it is claimed that the Monroe Doctrine should be maintained because we have more interests in America than has Europe. "We are remote from Europe; we are close to South America." Therefore, it is natural that we should have more interest than England or Germany in maintaining a benevolent protection over the fortunes of the Latin-American republics. This may be true of the countries in the vicinity of the Caribbean Sea, but it is far from true of the larger republics of South America. Their great cities are geographically nearer Europe than they are to the United States. Their population contains at least a million Italian immigrants, and many hundreds of thousands of Spanish, Portuguese, French, Germans, and English. While there are probably fewer French than those of any other nationality, the French actually outnumber the citizens of the United States who are living in the larger republics. Consequently, if there is any weight whatever in the fact that a nation has interests in a country where its citizens are employed, our interests are less than those of almost any one of the larger European countries. So far as investments are concerned, there is also no question whatever but that Europe has far more of a claim to be directly interested in the present state and future of the South American republics than has the United States. Compared to the hundreds of millions which England has invested in Argentina and Brazil, for instance, our own investments in those countries are ridiculously small. Consequently, this argument falls of its own weight, for to it we can reply that the larger and more important part of South America is nearer in miles, nearer in days of traveling, closer in ties of relationship, and more directly interested in commercial intercourse with Europe than with the United States.

The third argument is that the Monroe Doctrine has done South America a great deal of good in preventing her from being partitioned, as was Africa. Therefore, let us preserve it in all its pristine strength! It is quite true that the Monroe Doctrine undoubtedly protected South America against European aggression during a large part of the nineteenth century, when such aggression might have been fatal to the independence of several South American republics. But such a condition of affairs no longer exists, and if it should arise, that is to say if Germany should attempt to seize part of Brazil, for instance, or if Japan or China should attempt to coerce Peru into receiving undesirable immigrants, the best course for us to pursue would be, not to step forth single-handed as we did in 1823, but to join hands with the leading nations of South America in protecting the New World from the aggression of the Old. It is replied by some that this is merely a modification of the Monroe Doctrine. Insofar as it aims to accomplish certain results, that is true; insofar as it is promulgated in a different spirit and with a direct recognition of the actual state of our southern neighbors, it is different. Taking into account the extremely unpleasant connotation, in the ears of our southern neighbors, of the word Monroeism, we should be in a much stronger position if we would put that word aside, and adopt a new one, such as Pan-American Defense, which shall have for its connotation America for Humanity, and not America for the North Americans.

Having considered the chief arguments for retaining the

Monroe Doctrine, let us now briefly sum up the reasons why we should abandon it. First, the original Monroe Doctrine has been disregarded in several historical instances, notably after our war with Mexico in 1847 [1848], after our war with Spain in 1898, and in our dealings with Colombia, Santo Domingo, and Nicaragua. Second, owing to the constitutional changes that have taken place in the leading European nations since 1823, there is no danger that, in the words of President Monroe, the allied powers will "extend their political system to any portion of either continent." The world has advanced since then and the European nations themselves would be the first to object to any one of their number seizing a Latin-American republic, or setting up a monarchy there. Third, several of the South American states, notably Argentina, Brazil, and Chile, having attained their majority are no longer infants, do not need our protection, and will make better friends and stronger allies if we cease to hold the Monroe Doctrine as one of the tenets of our political faith. Fourth, their friendship is worth having. They are already building super-dreadnoughts, and, with our more extended frontier, and our outlying ports, such as Panama and Honolulu, we need cordial friends in the Western Hemisphere, and cannot afford to treat them in such a way as to estrange their sentiments. Fifth, the later form of the Monroe Doctrine, sometimes known as the "Big stick policy," or the "American policeman idea," by which we say to Europe that we cannot allow her to take any active interest in the political affairs of the Western Hemisphere, and accept the corresponding responsibility to look after her people and her property in the less well established republics, is a policy likely to involve us in tremendous difficulties and possibly in costly wars. It is a policy from which we have nothing to gain, and in which we have everything to lose. It is a policy which is likely to cost us the friendship not only of our American neighbors but, what is really of more importance to us, our European neighbors. Sixth, we should give up the Monroe Doctrine because the premises on which it was founded, and on which it was justified, no longer exist.

Today Europe has more citizens in South America than we have. She has invested a far larger share of her capital in South America than we have. She is bound to South Amer ica, not only by these ties of brotherhood and of property, but also by the racial ties which bind together the Latin race.

Geographically, Europe is nearer the chief cities of South America than is the United States; racially, she is closer; practically, she has more business interests there, and more of her sons are living there; and, finally, Europe has no intention of enforcing arbitrary monarchy and despotism on American states any more than we have.

As the premises on which the Monroe Doctrine was based no longer exist, and as the maintenance of our adherence to those words is of harm rather than good to us, it must be evident that the time has arrived for us to abandon this national shibboleth, and to clear the way for a new and logical foreign policy.

. . . . .

A DEFENSIVE ALLIANCE
FOR THE AMERICAS

Baltasar Brum

The Pan-Americanization of the Monroe Doctrine was urged by the President of Uruguay, Dr. Baltasar Brum (1883–1933), in an address delivered at the University of Montevideo in 1921, emphasizing the solidarity of the Americas and their need to defend themselves not only against the United States but also against extra-continental nations. Dr. Brum served as Uruguay's Minister of Foreign Affairs from 1915 to 1919 and as President of his country from 1919 to 1923. He did much to increase Uruguay's prestige abroad and gave clear exposition to the importance of Pan-American solidarity during World War I.

It can be stated that European conquests in America up to the present have been prevented by the influence of the Monroe Doctrine. Neither in the nineteenth century nor in the early decades of this century has there existed in Europe any power sufficiently strong to dare to annex American

Quoted in Félix Pérez Porta, "La Doctrina de Monroe," *Cuba Contemporánea*, Havana, XXVIII (January, 1922), 48–50. Translated by the editor.

territories at the cost of a war with the United States. I do not mean to say that they were not stronger than this country; rather, because of the rivalries among the nations of the Old World, none would have dared to provoke the United States, for such a situation would have been taken advantage of by its traditional enemies.

Under these conditions such attempts at conquest would have turned out to be difficult, bloody, and costly, and for that reason the expansionist-minded peoples of Europe have preferred to meet their needs and their aspirations by means of easier methods which offered them the helpless territories of Africa, Asia, or Oceania, and which moreover possessed great natural riches.

In that way throughout the past the Monroe Doctrine has served as an effective safeguard of the territorial integrity of many American countries. And it acquired a character of vital importance when the Pan-German propaganda, based on the military preparedness of Germany, revealed the possibility that that power in the event of a war victory in Europe—which would destroy the war effectiveness of its rivals and would free it from all worries about them—might determine to undertake the conquest of rich American countries, without fearing the force of the government at Washington.

The German threat to the territorial integrity of Latin America, already outlined in 1914 and in 1917, became clearer in 1918 when the German offensives of March and April—and the entrance of the United States into the war—came to have a significance anticipated by the Monroe Doctrine aimed not only at the defense of the United States but also at that of all the peoples of America, imperilled by the ambition of Pan-Germanism.

Uruguay understood the gravity of that historic moment and did not hesitate to ally itself with North America.

Because of the situation of the European powers since the war it can be stated that the danger of conquests by them in America has been postponed for many years.

But is that a reason why we should lose our interest in it for the future and should repudiate the Monroe Doctrine on the pretext that now we no longer need it?

I say no. Today more than ever before we ought to show foresight and search for formulas which will assure peace for all time and the complete independence of the American nations. To achieve this result we must intensify and deepen our feelings of solidarity.

The Monroe Doctrine is the only permanent expression of solidarity of one American country with the other countries of the continent. And I say this because it is the only one which has survived for a century, and other expressions of solidarity which other countries have formulated only respond to the political requirements of the historic moment and later generations have not considered themselves obliged to maintain them as directive norms of their foreign policy.

It is said that the Monroe Doctrine only responds to the selfish interests of the United States and that it is in a sense annoying to the American nations because it establishes something like a protectorate over them.

I consider that it is not reasonable to enter upon an investigation as to whether or not generous acts benefit the country which performs them. They can involve and almost always do involve an interested conclusion, although it may be only a moral judgment, and in this way they lose their intrinsic value. The only thing that ought to be considered, then, is the good that they produce.

According to the Monroe Doctrine, if an extracontinental power should undertake to conquer an American country, the latter could count on the aid of the nation of Washington.

Is not this a good for all? Is it not a practical and effective expression of true solidarity?

It has been stated by enemies of the Monroe Doctrine that such an attitude of the United States could wound the susceptibility of the country which has been attacked, that it would find itself protected without asking to be protected. But aside from the fact that this observation cannot be taken seriously this objection can be overcome if the American countries will formulate a declaration similar to that of Monroe, agreeing to intervene on behalf of each other, including the United States, in case they find themselves engaged in a war in defense of their rights with any extracontinental nation.

A declaration of that sort incorporated in the international engagements of each country would create for all a situation of great dignity and would place them on a plane of perfect moral equality with the United States. Its practical application would be as follows: if Uruguay, for example, should be attacked by an overseas power the United States and the other American nations would intervene in its defense, and if the attacker were the United States Uruguay together with its other brother [nations] of the continent would unite in action against the unjust aggressor.

So, the Monroe Doctrine, proclaimed as an actual norm of the foreign policy of the United States alone, would be transformed into a defensive alliance of all the American nations, based on a lofty sentiment of solidarity, with reciprocal obligations and advantages for all of them.

THE MONROE DOCTRINE

OFFICIALLY DEFINED

Charles Evans Hughes

Since John Quincy Adams, many Secretaries of State have officially defined what the Monroe Doctrine is and what it is not. Secretary of State Charles Evans Hughes (1862–1948) undertook this task in an address, "Observations on the Monroe Doctrine," delivered before the American Bar Association at Minneapolis, Minnesota, on August 30, 1923, printed below in part.

Hughes was nominated as the Republican candidate for the Presidency of the United States in 1916 but was defeated by Woodrow Wilson. He served as Secretary of State in the Cabinets of Presidents Warren G. Harding and Calvin Coolidge from 1921 to 1925. The views on the Monroe Doctrine set forth in the following address were a basis for the views which Hughes expressed as chairman of the United States delegation to the Sixth Inter-American Conference at Havana, Cuba, in 1928. From 1930 to 1941 Hughes served as Chief Justice of the United States.

Charles Evans Hughes, *The Pathway of Peace: Representative Addresses Delivered During His Term as Secretary of State (1921–1925)* (New York and London: Harper & Brothers, 1925), pp. 119–141. Reprinted by permission of the publisher.

. . . . .

The Monroe Doctrine is not a legislative pronouncement; it has been approved by action of Congress, but it does not rest upon any Congressional sanction. It has had the implied indorsement of the treaty-making power in the reservations to the two Hague conventions of 1899 and 1907, but it is not defined by treaty and does not draw its force from any international agreement. It is not like a constitutional provision deriving its authority from the fact that it is a part of the organic law transcending and limiting executive and legislative power. It is not a part of international law, maintained by the consent of the civilized powers and alterable only at their will. It is a policy declared by the Executive of the United States and repeated in one form and another by Presidents and Secretaries of State in the conduct of our foreign relations. Its significance lies in the fact that in its essentials, as set forth by President Monroe and as forcibly and repeatedly asserted by our responsible statesmen, it has been for 100 years, and continues to be, an integral part of our national thought and purpose, expressing a profound conviction which even the upheaval caused by the Great War and our participation in that struggle upon European soil has not uprooted or fundamentally changed.

Taking the Doctrine as it has been, and as it is believed to remain, I desire to comment upon certain points which, as I believe, deserve special emphasis at this time.

First, the Monroe Doctrine is not a policy of aggression; it is a policy of self-defense. It was asserted at a time when the danger of foreign aggression in this hemisphere was very real, when the new American states had not yet established a firm basis of independent national life, and we were menaced by threats of Old World powers directed against republican institutions. But the achievements of the century have not altered the scope of the Doctrine or changed its basis. It still remains an assertion of the principle of national security. As such, it is obviously not exclusive. Much time has been wasted in the endeavor to find in the Monroe Doctrine either justification, or the lack of it, for every governmental declaration or action in relation to other American states. Appropriate action for our defense may always be taken, and our proper influence to promote peace and good will may always be exerted, with the use of good offices to that end, whether or not the particular exigency comes within the range of the specific declarations which constitute the Doctrine.

In 1912, the Senate of the United States adopted a resolution apparently having immediate reference to Magdalena Bay

> that when any harbor or other place in the American continent is so situated that the occupation thereof for naval or military purposes might threaten the communications or the safety of the United States, the government of the United States could not see without grave concern possession of such harbor or other place by any corporation or association which has such a relation to another government, not American, as to give that government practical power or control for naval or military purposes.

It was explained in debate that this resolution, while allied to the Monroe Doctrine, was "not necessarily dependent upon it, or growing out of it." It was said to rest "on the principle that every nation has a right to protect its own safety, and that if it feels that the possession by a foreign power for military or naval purposes of any given harbor or place is prejudicial to its safety, it is its duty as well as its right to interfere."

The decision of the question as to what action the United States should take in any exigency arising in this hemisphere is not controlled by the content of the Monroe Doctrine, but may always be determined on grounds of international right and national security as freely as if the Monroe Doctrine did not exist. The essential character of that Doctrine is found in its particularization, in the definite and limited application of the general principle relating to national safety to a particular set of circumstances; that is, in the assertion and maintenance of opposition to the encroachment by non-American powers upon the political independence of American states and to the extension by non-American powers of their control over American territory. And in this pronouncement, as a phase of our exercise of the right of self-defense, there is no hint, much less threat, of aggression on our part. Said President Roosevelt: "It is in no wise intended as hostile to any nation in the Old World.

Still less is it intended to give cover to any aggression by any New World power at the expense of any other."

Second, as the policy embodied in the Monroe Doctrine is distinctively the policy of the United States, the government of the United States reserves to itself its definition, interpretation, and application. This government has welcomed the recognition by other governments of the fact and soundness of this policy and of the appropriateness of its application from time to time. Great powers have signified their acquiescence in it. But the United States has not been disposed to enter into engagements which would have the effect of submitting to any other power or to any concert of powers the determination either of the occasions upon which the principles of the Monroe Doctrine shall be invoked or of the measures that shall be taken in giving it effect. This government has not been willing to make the Doctrine or the regulation of its enforcement the subject of treaties with European powers; and, while the United States has been gratified at expressions on the part of other American states of their accord with our government in its declarations with respect to their independence and at their determination to maintain it, this government in asserting and pursuing its policy has commonly avoided concerted action to maintain the Doctrine, even with the American republics. As President Wilson observed: "The Monroe Doctrine was proclaimed by the United States on her own authority. It always has been maintained and always will be maintained upon her own responsibility."

This implies neither suspicion nor estrangement. It simply means that the United States is asserting a separate national right of self-defense, and that in the exercise of this right it must have an unhampered discretion. As Mr. Root has pithily said: "Since the Monroe Doctrine is a declaration based upon the nation's right of self-protection, it cannot be transmuted into a joint or common declaration by American states or any number of them." They have, of course, corresponding rights of self-defense, but the right is individual to each.

Further, in its own declarations the United States has never bound itself to any particular course of conduct in case of action by other powers contrary to the principles announced. In any such event it is free to act according to its conception of the emergency and of its duty. Dana, commenting upon this point in 1866 (in his edition of Wheaton), said:

> The declarations do not intimate any course of conduct to be pursued in case of such interpositions, but merely say that they would be "considered as dangerous to our peace and safety" and as "the manifestation of an unfriendly disposition toward the United States," which it would be impossible for us to "behold with indifference," thus leaving the nation to act at all times as its opinion of its policy or duty might require.

This is equally true today, but it may be added that this carefully preserved freedom does not detract from the tenacity with which the Doctrine is held but, like the Doctrine itself, has been maintained as essential to our independence and security.

Third, the policy of the Monroe Doctrine does not infringe upon the independence and sovereignty of other American states. Misconception upon this point is the only disturbing influence in our relations with Latin-American states. Great republics, whose independent sovereignty has been safeguarded by the historic Doctrine, no longer fear the danger of encroachments and control by European powers, but look with apprehension at the expansion, vast resources, rapidly growing population, and formidable strength of the Republic of the North. They do not feel the need of protection against European powers, and the Monroe Doctrine is apt to be conceived, and criticized, as a suggestion of a policy of interference in their internal affairs.

．　．　．　．　．

The Monroe Doctrine does not attempt to establish a protectorate over Latin-American states. Certainly, the declaration that intervention by non-American powers encroaching upon the independence of American states will be regarded as dangerous to our own safety gives no justification for such intervention on our part. If such foreign interposition is deemed menacing to us, and our vigorous determination to oppose it serves to safeguard the independence of American states, they can have no just objection on that score, being the more secure to develop their own life without hindrance. The declaration against acquisition by non-

American powers of American territory even by transfer might seem, at first glance, to furnish some basis for objection (although plainly in the interest of the integrity of American states) as an interference with the right of cession —but even this theoretical objection disappears when we consider the ground of the declaration upon this point by the government of the United States. That ground is found in the recognized right which every state enjoys, and the United States no less than any other, to object to acts done by other powers which threaten its own safety. The United States has all the rights of sovereignty, as well as any other power; we have lost none of our essential rights because we are strong, and other American states have gained none either because of increasing strength or relative weakness. The maxim of the civil law—*sic utere tuo, ut alienum non laedas*—may be applied to states where their action threatens the safety of another state.

. . . . . .

The declaration of our purpose to oppose what is inimical to our safety does not imply an attempt to establish a protectorate any more than a similar assertion by any one of the great southern republics of opposition to conduct on the part of any of the others endangering its security would aim at the establishment of a protectorate. I utterly disclaim, as unwarranted, the observations which occasionally have been made implying a claim on our part to superintend the affairs of our sister republics, to assert an overlordship, to consider the spread of our authority beyond our own domain as the aim of our policy, and to make our power the test of right in this hemisphere. I oppose all such misconceived and unsound assertions or intimations. They do not express our national purpose; they belie our sincere friendship; they are false to the fundamental principles of our institutions and of our foreign policy which has sought to reflect, with rare exceptions, the ideals of liberty; they menace us by stimulating a distrust which has no real foundation. They find no sanction whatever in the Monroe Doctrine. There is room in this hemisphere, without danger of collision, for the complete recognition of that Doctrine and the independent sovereignty of the Latin-American republics.

Fourth, there are, indeed, modern conditions and recent events which cannot fail to engage our attention. We have grown rich and powerful, but we have not outgrown the necessity, in justice to ourselves and without injustice to others, of safeguarding our future peace and security. By building the Panama Canal we have not only established a new and convenient highway of commerce but we have created new exigencies and new conditions of strategy and defense. It is for us to protect that highway. It may also be necessary for us at some time to build another canal between the Atlantic and the Pacific oceans and to protect that. I believe that the sentiment of the American people is practically unanimous that in the interest of our national safety we could not yield to any foreign power the control of the Panama Canal, or the approaches to it, or the obtaining of any position which would interfere with our right of protection or would menace the freedom of our communications.

So far as the region of the Caribbean Sea is concerned, it may be said that if we had no Monroe Doctrine we should have to create one. And this is not to imply any limitation on the scope of the Doctrine, as originally proclaimed and as still maintained, but simply to indicate that new occasions require new applications of an old principle which remains completely effective. What has taken place of late years in the region of the Caribbean has given rise to much confusion of thought and misapprehension of purpose. As I have said, the Monroe Doctrine as a particular declaration in no way exhausts American right or policy; the United States has rights and obligations which that Doctrine does not define. And in the unsettled condition of certain countries in the region of the Caribbean it has been necessary to assert these rights and obligations as well as the limited principles of the Monroe Doctrine.

·   ·   ·   ·   ·

The difficulties of these republics, and of other countries in a similar condition, are due in no small measure to the lack of the development of their resources and to the absence of needed facilities of intercourse, such as highways and railroads. It is idle to expect stability unless it has a basis in education, in improved methods of agriculture and industry, and in the provision of instrumentalities of communication which give opportunities for reasonable economic satisfactions. Progress in these directions, however, cannot be achieved without the investment of capital, and this must be supplied from the outside until sufficient available wealth has been produced within these countries to permit their people to meet their own exigencies. It is not the policy of our government to make loans to other governments and the needed capital, if it is to be supplied at all, must be furnished by private organizations. This has given rise to much misunderstanding and baseless criticism. We have no desire to exploit other peoples; on the other hand, it is surely not the policy of this government to stand in the way of the improvement of their condition. It is an inescapable fact, however, that private capital is not obtainable unless investment is reasonably secure and returns are commensurate with risks. There are always abundant opportunities for financial enterprise in our own country and in other parts of the world on these terms. We thus have the difficulty that the instability of governments creates a hazard which private capital refuses to ignore, while that very instability can be cured only by the economic betterment which private capital alone can make possible.

It must also be remembered that the government of the United States has no power to compel its citizens to lend money or to fix the terms of their investment. Nor is it in a position to control the action of other governments who desire to borrow. In this situation our government endeavors by friendly advice to throw its influence against unfairness and imposition, and it has at times, with the consent of the parties—indeed, at their instance—agreed to a measure of supervision in the maintenance of security for loans which otherwise would have been denied or would have been made only at oppressive rates. But anyone who supposes that this helpful contact and friendly relation are either sought or used by the government of the United States for purposes of aggression or with the intention of dominating the affairs of these countries or their governments has slight knowledge of the aims and actual endeavors of the Department of State. We are not seeking to extend this relation but to limit it; we are aiming not to exploit but to aid; not to subvert, but to help in laying the foundations for sound, stable, and independent government. Our interest does not lie in controlling foreign peoples; that would be a policy of mischief and disaster. Our interest is in having prosperous, peaceful, and law-abiding neighbors with whom we can cooperate to mutual advantage.

Fifth, it is apparent that the Monroe Doctrine does not stand in the way of Pan-American cooperation; rather it affords the necessary foundation for that cooperation in the independence and security of American states. The basis of Pan-Americanism is found in the principles of the Farewell Address. There was striking prophecy in the hope expressed by Jefferson that we would recognize "the advantages of a cordial fraternalization among all the American nations" and in what he described as "the importance of their coalescing in an American system of policy." That system is not hostile to Europe; it simply conserves the opportunity for the cultivation of the interests which are distinctively American.

. . . . .

Finally, it should be observed that the Monroe Doctrine is not an obstacle to a wider international cooperation, beyond the limits of Pan-American aims and interests, whenever that cooperation is congenial to American institutions. From the foundation of the government we have sought to promote the peaceful settlement of international controversies. Prior to the first peace conference at The Hague in 1899, the United States had participated in fifty-seven arbitrations. The United States became a party to the two Hague conventions for establishment of the Permanent Court of Arbitration, at the same time safeguarding its historic position by stating, as a part of the ratification, that nothing contained in these conventions should "be so construed as to require the United States of America to depart from its traditional policy of not entering upon, interfering with, or entangling itself in the political questions or internal administration of any foreign states" or "be construed to imply relinquishment by the United States of its traditional attitude toward purely American questions."

. . . . .

Our attitude is one of independence, not of isolation. Our people are still intent upon abstaining from participation in the political strife of Europe. They are not disposed to commit this government in advance to the use of its power in unknown contingencies, preferring to reserve freedom of action in the confidence of our ability and readiness to respond to every future call of duty. They have no desire to put their power in pledge, but they do not shirk cooperation with other nations whenever there is a sound basis for it and a consciousness of community of interest and aim. Cooperation is not dictation, and it is not partisanship. On our part it must be the cooperation of a free people drawing their strength from many racial stocks, and a cooperation that is made possible by a preponderant sentiment permitting governmental action under a system which denies all exercise of autocratic power. It will be the cooperation of a people of liberal ideals, deeply concerned with the maintenance of peace and interested in all measures which find support in the common sense of the country as being practicable and well designed to foster common interests.

To such aims the Monroe Doctrine is not opposed, and with the passing of 100 years it remains a cherished policy, inimical to no just interest and deemed to be vitally related to our own safety and to the peaceful progress of the peoples of this hemisphere.

AN INTER-AMERICAN
DOCTRINE

Alejandro Álvarez

The Latin-American origins and basis of the Monroe Doctrine were stressed by the Chilean specialist in international law Alejandro Álvarez (1868–1960). Professor of the history of law and comparative civil law at the University of Chile, he represented Chile at many international conferences and is the author of nearly 100 important works in the field of international law. The following selection is taken from his book *The Monroe Doctrine: Its Importance in the International Life of the States of the New World* (1924).

The principles contained in the celebrated Doctrine condense the ideas and aspirations which have sprung up and developed throughout the entire continent since the beginning of its independence.

· · · · ·

Alejandro Álvarez, *The Monroe Doctrine: Its Importance in the International Life of the States of the New World,* Carnegie Endowment for International Peace (New York: Oxford University Press, 1924), pp. 8–10, 19–21, 204–206. Reprinted by permission of the Carnegie Endowment for International Peace.

Before the former Spanish colonies severed their ties with the mother country, their leaders were already, without previous consultation with one another, full of ideas relating to their independence, to their future political organization, and to the relations they should maintain among themselves and with the countries of Europe.

The earliest ideas, which were also the clearest and most precise, were expressed in 1810, at a time when the movement for Spanish American independence had not yet openly begun, by the noted statesman Juan de Egaña in the "Project of a Declaration of Rights of the People of Chile." From that time, and especially since 1813, when the said movement had already begun, those same ideas were upheld with great ardor by statesmen of the different colonies in the struggle, principally by the great liberator, Bolívar, in various documents, prominent among which is his celebrated and prophetic "Letter from Jamaica," written in 1815. In 1817 the Liberator spoke for the first time of the "American pact."

From 1810 to 1815 the Latin-American ideas, called by some publicists the "Bolívar Doctrine," but which it would be more appropriate to call the "Egaña-Bolívar Doctrine," relate to the independence of the states of the New World and may be summarized as follows:

The Spanish-American colonies, in concert and mutually aiding each other, should free themselves from the mother country by force of arms, forming independent, sovereign states with a liberal, democratic, and constitutional government.

Moreover, the new states should form a confederation with common interests; those states should likewise be bound by close ties to the countries of Europe.

After 1815, through fear of intervention by the Holy Alliance, the earlier ideas (or doctrine) were modified and supplemented with new formulas, which may be summed up as follows:

The states of Latin America form an international society distinct from that of Europe; all the states must combine in a confederation, in order to proclaim their independence and to prevent the mother country or any other European state from oppressing them or standing in the way of their destinies.

In this confederation, moreover, adequate means must be provided for maintaining peace and settling disputes by arbitration. The relations between the confederated countries must be governed by principles of law in harmony with the new conditions and needs of those states.

The Spanish-American ideas (or doctrine) have points of contact with the Monroe ideas (or doctrine), as well as differences therefrom, which it may be useful to emphasize.

The Spanish-American ideas were enunciated before the former colonies had established their independence, at a time when everything depended upon their united efforts; the Monroe message appeared after they had attained that independence and the United States had recognized it. Both make the following declarations: (a) the nations of the New World have an acquired right to independence, which the countries of Europe cannot dispute; (b) the American continent is not susceptible of colonization in future; (c) the countries of Europe cannot extend to the New World the system of equilibrium, the basis of European politics prevailing at that time; (d) the countries of Europe cannot intervene in order to suppress or change the form of government of the new states, nor mix in their foreign affairs, nor control their destinies in any manner whatsoever.

Besides, both doctrines—the Monroe and the Latin-American—coincide in establishing, although implicitly, the *political equality* of all the countries.

The differences between the two doctrines are also clear: As we have said, Monroe did not attempt to formulate a doctrine, properly speaking, and when he made his declarations, he had chiefly in view the national interest; while the Latin statesmen tend to establish a true doctrine, taking into account national and continental interests. Moreover, the Latin states recognize that there is a close bond of solidarity between them and that consequently an offense against one of them is an offense against all, which all should punish. Finally, those same states, by virtue of this solidarity, manifest the desire to confederate, or form a society of nations governed above all by juridical principles.

In the Monroe Doctrine declarations are made with respect to the European colonies already established in America and to the intention of the United States not to meddle in the affairs of the Old World, points upon which the Latin doctrine makes no express declarations, since there was no necessity of doing so; but the ideas of the statesmen of Latin America on this subject were undoubtedly the same as those of the United States.

As regards those points on which the two doctrines coincide, they have a *continental character;* in the other points they are merely a *policy* of the United States or of the countries of Latin America.

Henceforth, therefore, the three great principles contained in Monroe's message are not merely a *policy* of the United States, but a *legal international doctrine,* because they have been affirmed by all the states of the New World.

. . . . .

Almost at the same time that the Monroe Doctrine was proclaimed, the United States inaugurated its imperialistic policy, or policy of territorial expansion on the continent. In the middle of the century, after the war with Mexico (1848), its territory was extended to the Pacific Ocean. This circumstance, together with the development of American commerce, gave birth to a new policy on the part of the United States—the policy of hegemony or supremacy—which consists in the intervention or control, in certain cases, of this country over the countries of Central America and those situated in or bordering on the Caribbean Sea. Presidents and Secretaries of State began to consider this policy of hegemony as a natural complement of the Monroe Doctrine, and to include it under this designation; the politicians and publicists did likewise. In 1856 Senator Bell of Tennessee said that the Monroe Doctrine had "become a doctrine of progressive absorption and annexation and conquest of Spanish America."

The Latin-American countries have always manifested frank opposition, as well as great anxiety, on account of that policy of the United States, and upon more than one occasion have formed alliances to defend themselves from it. The fact too that the United States has called this policy the "Monroe Doctrine" has given rise in the other American republics to a great aversion to the Doctrine, for they look upon it ordinarily no longer under the aspect which it had in 1823 but under the new aspect which has been given it.

In the course of the nineteenth century the policy of hegemony of the United States passed through various phases, which it may be useful to indicate:

1. The United States upon various occasions has claimed that a European state cannot, without the consent of the former, transfer to another European state the colonies which she possesses in the New World. (Declaration of Secretary Clay in 1825 to the governments of France and England that the Union would not permit Spain to transfer Cuba and Puerto Rico to another European country; declaration of President Grant in 1870 and of Secretary Fish in the same year to the effect that the time would come when the entire American continent would be absolutely free by voluntary relinquishment on the part of European countries of the colonies which they there possess.)

2. The policy followed with respect to Cuba from the beginning of the nineteenth century, while it was a colony. In regard to this policy, it is worth noting the declaration which was made in 1870 that the United States would look with disapproval upon Spain's contracting loans with the revenue coming from Cuba as a guaranty, Cuba being one of her colonies at the time.

3. Intervention at the birth of a new state on the continent, by emancipation or secession, afterwards restricting its external sovereignty. That is what happened in the case of Cuba and of Panama.

4. Intervention of the United States in the foreign affairs of certain Latin-American states when the territorial integrity of those countries was threatened. The two most conspicuous cases were its intervention in 1895 in the dispute between Venezuela and England regarding the boundary of Guiana, and the Anglo-Italo-German intervention in Venezuela in 1903 [December 1902]. In the first case, the Congress of the United States adopted on January 10, 1895, a resolution inviting the two parties to look with favor upon a proposal that they resort to arbitration.

5. Intervention in the internal affairs of certain Latin-American states in case of insurrection, especially in Cuba and Santo Domingo.

6. The control which the United States desires to exercise

over every interoceanic canal in the New World, for example the Panama Canal and the one planned across Nicaragua.

7. The policy proclaimed by President Roosevelt of exercising pressure against the Latin countries which fail to fulfill their international obligations, especially pecuniary obligations.

8. The control exercised by the United States over the economic life of certain countries to which it has loaned money to pay creditors; this situation is ordinarily regulated by treaties, for example with the Dominican Republic, with Nicaragua, etc.

Nevertheless it should be noted that the policy of hegemony does not go so far as to claim the right of assuming, at least directly, a protectorate over the countries of Latin America.

.   .   .   .   .

The Monroe Doctrine is not personal with regard to the United States; it represents the political and economic necessities of the American continent. If it has been considered a personal policy, the reason for this is the fact that it is found condensed in the message of 1823 and that the United States has been its champion.

We must mention again the mistaken belief that the Monroe Doctrine has served its time, for no state seriously disputes any longer the principles proclaimed therein. If this is true it is also true that the principles enunciated in it were bound to develop in accordance with the political necessities of the American continent.

This development is therefore the result of new circumstances and not of the flexibility of the declarations of 1823. In this development the Latin states have not always followed in line with the United States nor even with each other. Some of them were so far removed that they found themselves in a Utopia. We must therefore consider as a development or amplification of the Monroe Doctrine only the cases in which there has been an agreement between the Latin states and the United States and in which the latter has been disposed to make the Doctrine effective. This agreement came about in a clear and precise manner for the purpose of avoiding the occupation in any way whatsoever by the states of Europe of parts of American territory or of avoiding attempts on the part of the European states to acquire parts of these territories or to place them under their protectorate.

. . . . .

The truth is that the United States, while being an ardent defender of the Monroe Doctrine and its amplifications, has at the same time developed a personal policy which does not interpret and explain the sentiments of all America, namely, the policy of hegemony.

Hegemony consists of assuring its preponderance when its interests are at stake; accordingly it is a policy for its exclusive benefit. It consists also of intervention in certain internal or international affairs of some states. Furthermore, inspired by its present or future interests, it also pursues a noble object: the respect and good name of Latin America.

It intervenes in internal affairs by reason of a desire for peace which is advantageous to all; in international affairs it intervenes because of a desire for justice in favor of the weak states unjustly attacked and also in order to prevent them from committing with impunity acts that are reprehensible with regard to Europe.

This policy of hegemony is practiced almost exclusively on the countries that are the immediate neighbors of the United States, those bordering on the Gulf of Mexico (with the exception of Mexico) and those situated on the Caribbean Sea or located near it. This fact has given rise to the saying, not without reason, that the United States has made "an American lake" of the Gulf of Mexico.

It seeks to expand in these regions its economic interests, which are already more important than those of Europe. Besides, these states are weak; internally they are constantly troubled by civil wars, [and] the claims of the European states are numerous and sometimes followed by threats. The United States considers these acts as dangerous to its interest and to that of all America.

The policy of hegemony is the inevitable result of the tremendous and rapid development of the United States and of its enormous territorial, economic, and maritime superiority as compared with the other American republics. What has contributed to the success of this policy is the fact that it [the United States] has always presented it as a logical consequence of the Monroe Doctrine and that the powerful states, far from combating it, have always respected it. And it is interesting to state that, in certain cases in which the Monroe Doctrine might have been justly invoked, the United States did not do so and that on the other hand it invoked it for acts of hegemony in order to make them appear as being the outcome of a policy which is traditional and already admitted almost without dispute. It is this attitude which to a great extent has permitted the publicists to make no distinction between the two policies.

AN ALL-AMERICAN DOCTRINE

Simón Planas-Suárez

From 1904 to 1925, Simón Planas-Suárez (1879–), represented his country, Venezuela, in diplomatic posts in Austria, Italy, Greece, Holland, Hungary, Portugal, Rumania, and Yugoslavia. He has written many books in both the Spanish and the French languages in the fields of international law and international relations including, specifically, *L'Extension de la Doctrine de Monroe en Amérique du Sud* (1925) and *La Doctrina de Monroe y la Doctrina de Bolívar, los grandes principios de la política internacional Americana* (1925). He has been decorated by many foreign governments and has been honored by membership in dozens of learned societies in Venezuela and many other countries. In the pages that follow, Venezuela's most eminent "Monroísta" gives a favorable interpretation and comprehensive summary of the advantages of the Monroe Doctrine to Latin America.

Simón Planas-Suárez, *L'Extension de la Doctrine de Monroe en Amérique du Sud*, in Académie de Droit International, Recueil des Cours, 1924, IV, Tome 5 de la Collection (Paris: Librairie Hachette, 1925), pp. 273–274, 278–279, 327, 343–344, 352. Translated by the editor, and reprinted by permission of the Hague Academy of International Law.

The declarations formulated by President Monroe, in the name of the doctrine of national security, which all the American nations have proclaimed, are the fundamental affirmation of the right of the states of the New World to sovereign and independent existence and the basis of their principles of public law and of international American law. These declarations still embody the true sentiments of all the peoples of the continent; they are, as it were, the moral tie which unites the citizens of America in a common aspiration for a life of liberty, independence, and democracy: this is the obvious reason for the durability of the declarations of President Monroe.

Consequently, the Doctrine which bears his name preserves today all its value and cannot in any way be regarded from the general American viewpoint as out of date. On the contrary, to the extent that the American ideal becomes self-conscious and advances; to the extent that American brotherhood acquires more force; to the extent that [inter-American] relations become closer, thanks to better inter-American understanding; to the extent that commercial interchanges among the countries of the continent increase and their means of communication improve; in short, to the extent that Pan-Americanism grows and gains prestige, the Monroe Doctrine, or rather the principles intrinsically American and continental which have given vitality to it and which a century has only reinforced, acquires a new radiance and the power which is derived only from the strongest force that can sustain a principle, namely, the conscience of a people. And the conscience of the citizens of the New World is filled with the profound sentiment of liberty and of harmony, of independent sovereignty and of juridical and political equality, and of republican democracy which constitutes the essence of the American principles which President Monroe set forth to the world in a manner at once energetic, authoritative, and appropriate.

. . . .

The principles of which the Monroe Doctrine is the symbol therefore constitute for all America an essential element in its aspirations, for, in short, it is nothing but the theory of continental solidarity, a solidarity less narrow, naturally, than that which unites members of the same nation but is based on the notion of common interests and common dangers. . . .

Several writers of both hemispheres, without knowing the essence of the principles from which the Monroe Doctrine issued, charge that it is a creature of the United States and that it constitutes in United States hands a sort of instrument of protectorate instead of belonging to the whole of America. There is no supposition more absurd for one who knows its foundations. When one penetrates into the American spirit and ideal, it appears, with all the strength which the evidences of history furnish, that the American republics, without exception, have proclaimed the Doctrine without giving it a special name, for independent sovereignty, the territorial integrity of the American states, and the principle of non-intervention are called not the Monroe Doctrine but Pan-Americanism or, rather, the American doctrine or principles: names which are more general, without doubt, more universal, if this is possible, but which embody essentially the same aspirations and the same rights as those which President Monroe proclaimed.

. . . . . .

The situation that exists today is exactly the same as the situation that formerly existed: the Latin-American republics are still in their period of growth and development; they are still not powers of the first order in either wealth or material force, although some visionaries may think otherwise, but all of them are of the first order in the matter of desire for the progress of their peoples and in their patriotic feelings which will resist attempts against their liberty, their independence, and their sovereignty, and will defend their natural and legitimate right to shape their own destinies.

For this reason they are willing that the United States, as the strong Federation of the North, should make its powerful voice heard in the world, for Latin America is still too weak to do so. This is the only difference between North America and South America—the expression to all the other civilized powers of the earth of the American ideal, or, if you prefer, of the general political principles which concern the integrity of the rights of the American hemisphere, an integrity which all the sovereign and independent republics of the New World, whether jointly or separately, ought always to safeguard.

For, in summary, the declarations contained in the celebrated message of 1823 express, in a restrained form, the great continental principles proclaimed and defended by the founders of the American nations from the beginning of the struggle for independence of the new nationalities, principles which found great and universal expression in the famous Doctrine of Bolívar.

The Monroe Doctrine, in its original significance, is an American doctrine, it sets forth American principles, and consequently one ought not to say that it applies to such and such part of the American world, for its foundations were laid by all of America.

Some [Latin Americans] consider it a menace to the sovereignty and independence of our republics, others, on the contrary, as a blessing, necessary and indispensable to the maintenance of their independent sovereignty and their territorial integrity. The latter even go so far as to insist that the Monroe Doctrine ought to be *adopted* by the American republics or be extended to them.

The first point of view is erroneous, as one can easily see from the preceding chapters, which show the great American principles proclaimed and defended by all the republics of the continent, such as those of independence, of non-intervention, of territorial integrity, of juridical and political equality, and of continental solidarity. These principles can be summarized as principles of defense and security, invoked by the United States as being the very essence of the Monroe Doctrine, which is an affirmation, in the fullest sense, of the independent sovereignty of the American republics and the basis, consequently, of the principle of inter-American politics accepted by all the nations of the New World.

Such is the authentic Monroe Doctrine, according to the true spirit of the original proclamation, and it can have consequently no other meaning for the American republics.

As for the politics of imperialism or hegemony practiced on certain occasions by the government of Washington and against which all the republics to the south of the United States have protested and will always protest in the name of the principle of legitimate defense and of security which is the essential base of the Monroe Doctrine, . . . that policy has nothing to do with the Doctrine, as both Mr. Hughes and Mr. Root recognize. It is independent of it; it has developed under special conditions and in different situations.

. . . . .

The essential principles of the declarations of President Monroe which gave rise to the Doctrine are originally and fundamentally American. . . . These principles, which the United States has condensed in recent times into the expression "its own security and defense," are known by Anglo-Americans and by the world in general under the name of the Monroe Doctrine. It is a question then of a particular name, of a name which belongs, in fact and in law, to the United States, and we believe naturally that no other country of America has the right to adopt the name of Monroe Doctrine to describe the American principles which it proclaims as the rule of its international politics. For the same reasons it is equally impossible to speak of an *extension* of the Monroe Doctrine to the other American Republics.

. . . . .

LATIN-AMERICAN
OPPOSITION TO THE
NEW MONROEISM

Felipe Barreda y Laos

Felipe Barreda y Laos (1888–   ), former professor of Pan-American history at the University of San Marcos, Lima, Peru, in the following article analyzes the "deformations" of the Monroe Doctrine and gives suggestions for a return to "the original and undistorted" Doctrine. At the time he published the article, Señor Barreda was editor of *La República* of Lima. He later served as Peruvian Ambassador to Argentina and Uruguay (1930–1938) and represented Peru at the seventh Inter-American Conference at Montevideo in 1933.

The landing of American bluejackets in Nicaragua and the Mexican conflict over the enforcement of oil and land laws have not only given ground for criticism, but also once more caused discussion of the Monroe Doctrine. Superficial investigation and defective interpretation of the facts are responsible for the persistent distortion of that historic declaration both in the United States and in Latin America. My position as professor of Pan-American history, the first and

Felipe Barreda y Laos, "Latin American Opposition to the New Monroeism," *Current History*, XXV (March 1927), 809–812. Reprinted by permission of the publisher.

oldest chair of its kind in Latin America, which I established in the University of San Marcos, Lima, Peru, in 1910, necessitated my reading many books and articles by Latin-American writers on the Monroe Doctrine; and in almost all of them I found a startling misinterpretation of the facts.

In Latin-American countries the error prevails that the Monroe Doctrine was a sort of gift, emotional in character, which the United States presented to the new republics of this hemisphere as an expression of exalted and romantic sympathy in behalf of their struggle for independence. On the other hand, it is a common mistake among the people of the United States to appeal to the Monroe Doctrine as a ready excuse to justify armed intervention and political interference in Latin-American countries in behalf of commercial and industrial enterprises. These erroneous conceptions lead to misunderstanding and the growth of suspicion and animosity between the United States and Latin America.

The Monroe Doctrine was first of all and substantially a declaration by the United States for international self-protection and, what is very important, for the protection of its commerce and industries against European intrigues at a particular moment of American history. In this sense it was interpreted from 1823, when it was enunciated, until the time of the first McKinley administration, when a second period began during which the Doctrine was distorted and given a new meaning.

During the first period all the different applications of the Monroe Doctrine referred to the protection of the two Americas *against European interference* or threatened invasions. Such cases were: the dispute with Great Britain over the State of Oregon in 1848 [*sic*], the French invasion of Mexico in behalf of Maximilian, the controversy with Great Britain over the boundary between Venezuela and British Guiana, the claims of Italy against the Republic of Colombia, and various demands by European countries on Spanish-American republics regarding public debts. In all these questions the Monroe Doctrine was reaffirmed in its true character as a defense of America against *European* interference.

As the scope of the Doctrine was extended to South-American republics on so many different occasions, it assumed the form of a system of Pan-American protection of the highest moral and idealistic value. Monroeism came to mean continental freedom and civilization. For this reason all Latin-American countries rejoiced in and honored with the greatest enthusiasm the triumphal visit of Elihu Root, Secretary of State, in 1906. All the speeches made by both the Latin Americans and Mr. Root on that occasion went to prove that it was the original conception of Monroeism that inspired the new policy of Pan-Americanism. Monroeism and Pan-Americanism were, indeed, two complementary conceptions that could not be imagined at that time as likely to become antagonistic. Latin America had no grievances against the United States, nor the least reason for misgivings as to the future.

After the independence of Latin America was established, the United States was absorbed in its own internal development, and had no other attitude toward Latin America than that of friendship and political sympathy. But by the time President McKinley had been elected, the Colossus of the North had grown in stature and was rich, strong, and abounding in vitality. The American people rejoiced in their increasing prosperity, and when the Spanish-American War came and ended in victory they were strengthened in national spirit and the feeling of national unity. While rapidly accumulating surplus capital was looking for foreign markets and international expansion, Elihu Root's statesmanship pointed to the golden horizon of the Southern Continent. At the Trans-Mississippi Commercial Congress in Kansas City in 1906 he made clear the new direction which the industrial and commercial expansion of the nation should take.

Cuba and Puerto Rico as natural zones of expansion acquired in the Spanish-American War were succeeded by increasing investments in Central America and in every country of South America. Mines, oil, agriculture, roads, bridges, railroads, and national loans absorbed hundreds of millions of dollars each year, while commerce with the Southern Continent expanded correspondingly. During the last twenty years the people of the United States have invested in Latin America $4,210,000,000; trade with the United States has come to be represented by 18.5 percent of the total yearly exports of this country.

In the same period, coincidentally with this remarkable expansion, the Monroe Doctrine has been corrupted and distorted in such an extraordinary manner that both its interpretation and its application have no connection at all with the policy originally stated by President Monroe. The cause has been the friction and conflict growing out of commercial intercourse, and the result has been that, in order to find a line of solution, the United States government has made use of the Monroe Doctrine for its own purposes by drawing from it conclusions of the most variable and fantastic character. A study of various cases of the modern interpretation and application of the Doctrine in the last twenty years makes it clear that it has been employed in the following ways typical of the new conception which has superseded Monroe's own formulation of his ideas:

1. In cases of internal political strife or revolution in Latin-American countries the government of the United States assumes the right to declare which is the constitutional party to be supported by the military and naval power of the United States. (First intervention in Nicaragua, 1912.)

2. When the conclusion is reached that a Latin-American country is not able to maintain an independent and competent government to keep order and discharge its international obligations, the United States assumes the right to take political and economic control of such country. (Intervention in Haiti, 1915.)

3. The United States assumes the right to intervene in the political government and economic administration of a debtor nation in Latin America to enforce and secure the cancellation of public debts. (Santo Domingo, 1916.)

4. The United States government assumes the right to intervene in the internal affairs of Latin-American countries when, in its opinion, political or economic ideas may endanger the private interests of American citizens. (The controversy with Nicaragua and Mexico now in progress.)

5. The fixed attitude of the United States that the definition, interpretation, and application of the Monroe Doctrine are its exclusive concern.

These deformations of the Monroe Doctrine have nothing in common with President Monroe's declaration. They lack the essential character of Monroeism—defense against *European* intervention; they destroy the conception of a single continental front against the diplomatic intrigues of the world; they set the south against the north; and they are contradictory to the advice not only of Monroe but of such statesmen as Washington and Quincy Adams. . . .

. . . . . .

Inaugurated by Secretary of State Blaine in 1889, and developed by the eloquent support of Mr. Root, Pan-Americanism has been growing as a real spiritual and moral bond between American nations on the basis of better understanding and reciprocal aid in behalf of the civilization of the New World. Pan-Americanism endows every nation of the two Americas, no matter what is its size or power, with the same rights as were proclaimed a century and a half ago to the American democracy. Pan-Americanism means freedom for all time from all danger of political or economic imperialism or slavery, not international guardianship or dictation. Pan-Americanism is fraternity and association without privilege or discrimination, without pride of superiority on the one hand and humiliation, fear, or anxiety on the other. Pan-Americanism is not a method of propaganda for commercial intercourse; on the contrary, trade should be developed for the promotion of reciprocal economic interest and international sympathy in behalf of Pan-Americanism. Otherwise, the Pan American Union, which has its headquarters in Washington, should not exist and its functions would be better absorbed by the United States Chamber of Commerce. Pan-Americanism, with which the old and genuine Monroe Doctrine is in perfect accord, cannot coexist with Monroeism as it is interpreted today.

. . . . . .

To save Pan-Americanism from total wreck these suggestions are made:

1. The United States must return to the original and undistorted doctrine enunciated by President Monroe.

2. All the nations which form the Pan American Union must adopt the principle of no political interference between themselves on any excuse whatever. They also must adopt the principle of no military enforcement of agreements or contracts dealing with matters which do not fall within the scope of international law.

3. Every international conflict between two or more American states must be settled by the World Court.

No other interest must prevail than that of saving the results gained after twenty years' work for Pan-Americanism.

MEMORANDUM ON THE
MONROE DOCTRINE

J[oshua] Reuben Clark

The publication by the State Department in 1930 of
the *Memorandum on the Monroe Doctrine,* prepared
by Under Secretary of State J. Reuben Clark (1871–
1961), marked a turning point in the history and interpretation of the Doctrine. Clark served as Under
Secretary of State from 1928 to 1929, as Ambassador to
Mexico from 1930 to 1933, and as a member of the
United States delegation to the seventh Inter-American
Conference at Montevideo in 1933.

. . . . .

It is of first importance to have in mind that Monroe's declaration in its terms relates solely to the relationships between European states on the one side, and, on the other
side, the American continents, the Western Hemisphere,
and the Latin-American governments which on December
2, 1823, had declared and maintained their independence
which we had acknowledged.

Department of State, *Memorandum on the Monroe Doctrine,* prepared by J. Reuben Clark, Under Secretary of State, December 17,
1928 (Washington: Government Printing Office, 1930), pp. xix–xxv.

It is of equal importance to note, on the other hand, that the declaration does not apply to purely inter-American relations.

Nor does the declaration purport to lay down any principles that are to govern the interrelationship of the states of this Western Hemisphere as among themselves.

The Doctrine states a case of United States *vs.* Europe, not of United States *vs.* Latin America.

Such arrangements as the United States has made, for example, with Cuba, Santo Domingo, Haiti, and Nicaragua, are not within the Doctrine as it was announced by Monroe. They may be accounted for as the expression of a national policy which, like the Doctrine itself, originates in the necessities of security or self-preservation—a policy which was foreshadowed by Buchanan (1860) and by Salisbury (1895)—and was outlined in what is known as the "Roosevelt Corollary" to the Monroe Doctrine (1905) in connection with the Dominican debt protocol of 1904. But such arrangements are not covered by the terms of the Doctrine itself.

Should it become necessary to apply a sanction for a violation of the Doctrine as declared by Monroe, that sanction would run against the European power offending the policy, and not against the Latin-American country which was the object of the European aggression, unless a conspiracy existed between the European and the American states involved.

In the normal case, the Latin-American state against which aggression was aimed by a European power, would be the beneficiary of the Doctrine not its victim. This has been the history of its application. The Doctrine makes the United States a guarantor, in effect, of the independence of Latin-American states, though without the obligations of a guarantor to those states, for the United States itself determines by its sovereign will when, where, and concerning what aggressions it will invoke the Doctrine, and by what measures, if any, it will apply a sanction. In none of these things has any other state any voice whatever.

Furthermore, while the Monroe Doctrine, as declared, has no relation in its terms to an aggression by any other state than a European state, yet the principle "self-preservation" which underlies the Doctrine—which principle, as we shall

see, is as fully operative without the Doctrine as with it—
would apply to any non-American state in whatever quarter
of the globe it lay, or even to an American state, if the
aggressions of such state against other Latin-American
states were "dangerous to our peace and safety," or were a
"manifestation of an unfriendly disposition towards the
United States," or were "endangering our peace and happiness"; that is, if such aggressions challenged our existence.

In other words, there is a broad domain occupied by self-
preservation which is incapable of definite boundary as to
its extent, or of definition as to the kind of act which lies
within it, because new conditions, new advances in the arts
and sciences, new instrumentalities of international contact
and communication, new political theories and combinations, vary from age to age and cannot be certainly foretold.
As the law stands, whatever falls within the necessities of
self-preservation, under existing or future conditions, lies
within the boundaries of the domain of the principle.

By his declaration President Monroe occupied and
bounded but a narrow portion of this whole domain—that
portion which contained situations immediately threatening.
But that can hardly be said to have changed under the rules
and principles of international law the fundamental character of the acts defined and bounded. These acts still remained within the domain of self-preservation, for, obviously, if they would constitute a menace to our existence,
such menace would not disappear by virtue of their being
listed.

In this view, the Monroe Doctrine as such might be
wiped out and the United States would lose nothing of its
broad, international right; it would still possess, in common
with every other member of the family of nations, the inter-
nationally recognized right of self-preservation, and this
right would fully attach to the matters specified by the Doctrine if and whenever they threatened our existence, just as
the right would attach in relation to any other act carrying a
like menace.

The Doctrine has been useful, and such indeed was the
real motive of its announcement, and it will remain of such
use that it should never be abandoned, as a forewarning to
European powers as to what this country would regard, in a
restricted field, as inimical to its safety. It has been equally

useful to the Americas as forecasting our attitude towards certain international problems and relations in which they might be involved.

But, recalling that the Doctrine is based upon the recognized right of self-preservation, it follows (it is submitted) that by the specification of a few matters in the Doctrine, the United States has not surrendered its right to deal, as it may be compelled, and under the rules and principles of international law, with the many others which are unspecified as these may arise, which others might, indeed, have been included in the declaration with as much propriety, legally, as those which were mentioned. By naming either one act or a series of acts which challenges our self-preservation, we do not estop ourselves from naming others as they may arise; otherwise the mention of one such act would foreclose all others. The custom of nations shows that invoking the right as to one menace does not foreclose a power from invoking it as to others.

Moreover, by specifying a few of the world powers which, if they performed the prohibited acts, would bring themselves within the inhibitions of the Doctrine, the United States has not estopped itself from asserting the same principles against other and unnamed powers making the same sort of aggression. That against these other powers, the United States might, in its intervention, speak of the right of self-preservation and not of the Monroe Doctrine, would neither enlarge nor diminish its rights under international law as to the Monroe Doctrine or otherwise.

It is evident from the foregoing that the Monroe Doctrine is not an equivalent for "self-preservation"; and therefore the Monroe Doctrine need not, indeed should not, be invoked in order to cover situations challenging our self-preservation but not within the terms defined by Monroe's declaration. These other situations may be handled, and more wisely so, as matters affecting the national security and self-preservation of the United States as a great power.

It has been sometimes contended (see particularly the speech in the Senate by Senator Calhoun in 1848 regarding the situation in Yucatan) that the Doctrine was announced merely to meet the threatened aggressions of the European Alliance in 1823, and that the Doctrine became obsolete with the passing of this immediate threat. But this view is not supported by the language of the declaration which as to action *"by any European power"* (both as to colonization and interposition) is unlimited in time; nor by that part of the declaration which specifically mentions the *"allied powers,"* for here the declaration is couched in such general terms as to be, with sound reason, applied to any power or powers whatsoever who should, at any time, commit the aggressions against which the announced policy was aimed.

During the period since the Doctrine was announced there have been assertions at various times as to situations which were not objectionable to the Doctrine or to the principles underlying the same. In few of these instances has it been categorically asserted that the Monroe Doctrine did not cover the specific matter in question, the ruling or declaration having usually come in the form of a statement to the effect that some particular situation was not inimical to the interests of the United States.

The statement of the Doctrine itself that "with the existing colonies or dependencies of any European power we have not interfered and shall not interfere," has been more than once reiterated.

It has also been announced that the Monroe Doctrine is not a pledge by the United States to other American states requiring the United States to protect such states, at their behest, against real or fancied wrongs inflicted by European powers, nor does it create an obligation running from the United States to any American state to intervene for its protection.

Mr. Clay in 1828 asserted that the Monroe Doctrine was not applicable to wars as between American states, and it was likewise very early declared by Mr. Clay (1825) "that whilst the war is confined to the parent country and its former colony, the United States remain neutral, extending their friendship and doing equal justice to both parties."

Beginning in the second half of the last century (1861) the United States took the position that it would consider that Spain was "manifesting an unfriendly spirit toward the United States" if it should undertake the resubjection of certain of her former colonies, and this position was reiterated at later dates.

Commencing with 1825 and running on down through the whole of the last century it was repeatedly asserted that the Monroe Doctrine did not require the United States to prevent Europe from waging war against Latin-American countries, and from almost as early a period down to the close of the century the principle was followed (as announced by Secretary Sherman in 1898) that it was not the duty of the United States "to protect its American neighbors from the responsibilities which attend the exercise of independent sovereignty."

The United States has at times jointly intervened with European countries in internal situations existing in the Latin Americas; at other times it has declined to participate in such intervention.

A popular feeling exists that the Monroe Doctrine is hostile to monarchical government as such, but this is not the fact. Monarchies have been set up in Brazil, Haiti, and Mexico without objection by the United States, and for many years we dealt with the Brazilian monarchy on terms and in language of sincere friendship. Even the establishment of the Maximilian Empire in Mexico was objected to not so much from the point of view of its being a monarchy as from the point of view that this monarchy was established and maintained by European troops.

One of the interesting suggestions that have been made by European powers is that the possession of colonies by that power upon this hemisphere makes of that possessing power an American state. This suggestion has, of course, not been acceptable to the United States.

The Monroe Doctrine has always been considered as covering a possession—either "temporary or permanent" (Forsyth, 1840)—of American territory by European powers, and in line with that principle, we have declared that the Monroe Doctrine forbade the occupation of American territory by such powers. President Roosevelt in his message of February 15, 1905, in relation to the situation in Santo Domingo, declared:

> An aggrieved nation can without interfering with the Monroe Doctrine take what action it sees fit in adjustment of its disputes with American states, provided that action does not take the shape of interference with their form of government or of the despoilment of their territory under any disguise.

At various times proposals have been made that the United States should join with Europe in neutralizing certain areas (notably Cuba) on this continent, but the United States has steadily declined to join in such an action. One of the classic notes that have been written regarding the relationship between the United States and the other Americas was penned by Secretary Everett on December 1, 1852, regarding a proposal to neutralize Cuba.

The so-called "Roosevelt Corollary" was to the effect, as generally understood, that in case of financial or other difficulties in weak Latin-American countries, the United States should attempt an adjustment thereof lest European governments should intervene, and intervening should occupy territory—an act which would be contrary to the principles of the Monroe Doctrine. This view seems to have had its inception in some observations of President Buchanan in his message to Congress of December 3, 1860, and was somewhat amplified by Lord Salisbury in his note to Mr. Olney of November 6, 1895, regarding the Venezuelan boundary dispute.

As has already been indicated above, it is not believed that this Corollary is justified by the terms of the Monroe Doctrine, however much it may be justified by the application of the doctrine of self-preservation.

These various expressions and statements, as made in connection with the situations which gave rise to them, detract not a little from the scope popularly attached to the Monroe Doctrine, and they relieve that Doctrine of many of the criticisms which have been aimed against it.

Finally, it should not be overlooked that the United States declined the overtures of Great Britain in 1823 to make a joint declaration regarding the principles covered by the Monroe Doctrine, or to enter into a conventional arrangement regarding them. Instead this government determined to make the declaration of high national policy on its own responsibility and in its own behalf. The Doctrine is thus purely unilateral. The United States determines when and if the principles of the Doctrine are violated, and when and if violation is threatened. We alone determine what measures, if any, shall be taken to vindicate the principles of the Doctrine, and we of necessity determine when the principles have been vindicated. No other power of the world has any relationship to, or voice in, the implementing of the principles which the Doctrine contains. It is our Doctrine, to be by us invoked and sustained, held in abeyance, or abandoned as our high international policy or vital national interests shall seem to us, and to us alone, to demand.

It may, in conclusion, be repeated: The Doctrine does not concern itself with purely inter-American relations; it has nothing to do with the relationship between the United States and other American nations, except where other American nations shall become involved with European governments in arrangements which threaten the security of the United States, and even in such cases, the Doctrine runs against the European country, not the American nation, and the United States would primarily deal thereunder with the European country and not with the American nation concerned. The Doctrine states a case of the United States *vs.* Europe, and not of the United States *vs.* Latin America. Furthermore, the fact should never be lost to view that in applying this Doctrine during the period of 100 years since it was announced, our government has over and over again driven it in as a shield between Europe and the Americas to protect Latin America from the political and territorial thrusts of Europe; and this was done at times when the American nations were weak and struggling for the establishment of stable, permanent governments; when the political morality of Europe sanctioned, indeed encouraged, the acquisition of territory by force; and when many of the great powers of Europe looked with eager, covetous eyes to the rich, undeveloped areas of the American hemisphere. Nor should another equally vital fact be lost sight of, that the United States has only been able to give this protection against designing European powers because of its known willingness and determination, if and whenever necessary, to expend its treasure and to sacrifice American life to maintain the principles of the Doctrine. So far as Latin America is concerned, the Doctrine is now, and always has been, not an instrument of violence and oppression, but an unbought, freely bestowed, and wholly effective guaranty of their freedom, independence, and territorial integrity against the imperialistic designs of Europe.

A MEMORANDUM ON
INTER-AMERICAN
RELATIONS

Sumner Welles

Suggestions for a reformulation of United States policy toward Latin America in accordance with the revised conception of the Monroe Doctrine were made to President-elect Franklin D. Roosevelt in the following memorandum by Sumner Welles (1892–1961), who would soon, as Assistant Secretary of State and later Under Secretary of State in the Roosevelt administration, be given the responsibility of implementing the Good Neighbor Policy of that administration. Welles had already suggested some of these new lines of policy in the concluding chapter of his *Naboth's Vineyard* (1928).

The following memorandum was discovered among the Franklin D. Roosevelt papers by Professor Charles C. Griffin and is given here with his introduction as published originally in the *Hispanic American Historical Review*.

Sumner Welles to President-elect Franklin D. Roosevelt, 1933, edited with introductory comments by Charles C. Griffin, *Hispanic American Historical Review*, XXXIV (May, 1954), [90]–92. Reprinted by permission of the publisher.

In a recent letter Mr. Welles describes the circumstances in which this memorandum was written as follows:

> During the months between his nomination and his inauguration the President made it his practice to invite to visit him at Albany or at Hyde Park a group of advisors to review with him questions of domestic and foreign policy. I sent the President the memorandum of which you have sent me a copy as an outgrowth of one of those meetings during which questions of hemispheric policy were discussed. I had already for a good many years been given the opportunity of talking over questions of foreign policy with the President, particularly questions relating to inter-American relations.

The memorandum, therefore, represents in concise form the thinking of one of Franklin D. Roosevelt's most trusted advisers in the field of inter-American relations in the days immediately preceding the announcement of the "Good Neighbor Policy." It was part of the material from which the President and his speechwriting assistants drafted the inaugural address delivered on March 4, 1933. In that speech international relations were dealt with briefly and generally, but on Pan American Day, April 14, in the midst of his overwhelming domestic preoccupations, Roosevelt delivered an address in which some of the ideas presented in the Welles memorandum printed below were incorporated. Over-all development of the policy recommended by Welles was to occupy a large part of Roosevelt's first two presidential terms.

Students of inter-American relations will find it useful to be able to establish for a date as early as the beginning of 1933 the thinking of the Roosevelt administration on such policies as continental defense, the principle of inter-American consultation, and the reciprocal trade agreements program. Similarly, the position with regard to intervention, though in certain important details at variance from that adopted by the United States after the Montevideo Conference (1933), marks a sharp break with the policies followed by the United States during the preceding three decades.

Document

The creation and maintenance of the most cordial and intimate friendship between the United States and the other republics of the American Continent must be regarded as a keystone of our foreign policy. The erroneous interpretations given to the Monroe Doctrine over a period of many decades have constituted a constant cause for apprehension and for misrepresentation of the true purposes of the Government of the United States. The Monroe Doctrine declares that the United States will not permit any non-American nation to encroach upon the political independence of any American republic; and that the United States will not consent to the acquisition in any manner of the control of additional territory in this Hemisphere by any non-American Power. These principles have until now been proclaimed solely on the authority of the United States and they will not be abandoned. But they are essentially principles of continental self-defense. And they are as vitally important to every other republic of this Hemisphere as they are to the United States itself. I would welcome their adoption by every American republic as a portion of its national policy. In that manner alone, in my opinion, can there be permanently abolished the impression which has persisted that these simple principles of self-defense can involve a threat to the sovereignty or to the national well being of any republic of the Western Hemisphere. In the same spirit of mutual understanding and of cooperation for the promotion of the welfare of the American peoples, I favor the principle of consultation between the governments of the American republics whenever there arises in this continent any question which threatens the peace and well being of the American world. I believe that in such emergency there should be summoned immediately an inter-American conference, in which the American republics can determine, as individual powers bound together by a common interest, what policy best behooves them in a crisis which may be of potential danger to each of them in varying degree. The United States should take the ground that pan-American responsibilities must be accepted by all the American republics on equal terms. I would stress, in particular, the continental responsibility for the maintenance of peace in this Hemisphere, and the necessity for the perfection of the mechanism required for the carrying out of that obligation.

The lives of our citizens abroad must, of course, be protected, wherever they may be, when they are in imminent danger and the local authorities are patently unable to afford them security, but such protection by this government should never again result in armed intervention by the United States in a sister republic. I believe that the dispatch of the armed forces of the United States to any foreign soil whatsoever, save for the purpose of dealing with a temporary emergency such as that just described, should never be undertaken by the American Executive except with the consent of the American Congress.

There is no more effective means of enhancing friendship between nations than in promoting commerce between them. We cannot expect to preserve the sincere friendship of our neighbors on this Continent if we close our markets to them. We cannot enjoy the markets of the American Continent, which have as vast a potentiality for development as any in the world, unless we permit the citizens of our sister nations to trade with us. The interest of the peoples of this Continent demands that the American governments individually take without delay such action as may be necessary to abolish those barriers and restrictions which now hamper the healthy flow of commerce between their respective nations.

A "NEW DEAL"
IN PAN-AMERICANISM?

Raúl Díez de Medina [Gaston Nerval]

The "New Deal" in Pan-Americanism which was inaugurated by President Franklin D. Roosevelt in 1933
required the abandonment of the Monroe Doctrine, in
the opinion of the Bolivian diplomat and journalist
Raúl Díez de Medina (1909–   ), who wrote his indictment of the Doctrine under the pseudonym Gaston
Nerval. He served in the Bolivian legation in Washington in 1930 and at the time of this publication is serving
as Bolivian Ambassador to the Organization of American States.

. . . . .

The Monroe Doctrine, as interpreted by the successors of
President Monroe, has been the paramount feature of the
Latin-American policy of the United States. It has been
invoked to account for every action of this country in its
relations with the Southern Hemisphere. It has been, mali-
ciously or innocently, transformed, time and again, to fit the

Raúl Díez de Medina, *Autopsy of the Monroe Doctrine: the Strange
Story of Inter-American Relations* (New York: Macmillan Company,
1934), pp. 311–324.

different situations and support the United States in each separate emergency.

Because of that, the Monroe Doctrine is inexorably linked with the fate of inter-American relationships. In the eyes of Anglo-Saxon Americans, the Monroe Doctrine justifies all the aggressive policies of the past. In the eyes of Latin Americans, it is the pretext for them.

We have seen that most of the theories and practices employed by the United States in Latin America, and officially or tacitly admitted as justified under imaginary powers of an ever-changing Monroe Doctrine, not only have disregarded the law of nations, but have also been the source of bitter controversies, resentment, and suspicion between Anglo-Saxon and Latin in the Western Hemisphere. The various phases of United States hegemony and of United States intervention in Latin America—territorial expansion, *paramount interest, Manifest Destiny,* overlordship, intervention in foreign affairs, intervention in behalf of Europe, intervention for policing purposes, the policy of the *big stick, dollar diplomacy,* etc.—must, then, be eliminated before any real program for Pan-American harmony is attempted.

But the mere discontinuance of such practices is not enough. As a matter of fact, the trend of the Latin-American policy of the State Department, for the past few years, has been one of gradual drifting away from the much discredited practices of yesterday. But, who is to guarantee to the Latin Americans, made extremely skeptical by contradictions and unkept promises in the past, that this improvement is more than a temporary one? Who is to guarantee to them that the abuses apparently disavowed are not to be again indulged in the future, under some new interpretation, or a revived one, of the multiheaded *shibboleth* which, for over 100 years, has furnished an excuse for every inexcusable act of the United States in Latin America?

The only way to eliminate completely the ground for suspicion and the resentment today prevailing—a condition essential to the success of any Pan-American scheme—is to discard the *shibboleth* itself. The only way to assure the Latin Americans that the unfortunate theories and practices of the past will have no repetition—and thus regain their lost good will—is to abandon the instrument which has served to foster them; to give up, once for all, the fictitious

and self-imposed rights successively "discovered" with each
new interpretation of the Monroe Doctrine. The only way is
to renounce the Doctrine itself which, rightly or wrongly, is
so intimately associated with those practices and the peculiar theories which originated them.

Nor is it enough to state, at this eleventh hour, that the
Monroe Doctrine really had little to do with such things as
have been committed in its name, after the things *have been*
committed and the Doctrine *has been* given and accepted
for their explanation. High State Department officials have
tried this, recently, in a vain attempt to vindicate the Doctrine, even though this attempt amounted to a disavowal of
the past policies. They have advocated a return to the original Monroe Doctrine, probably to avoid responsibility for
the changes and distortions wrought by their predecessors.
But this can help only slightly. Individual declarations or
pledges of good intentions for the future cannot change
overnight the impression which 100 years of an elastic,
capricious, ever-changing Monroe Doctrine, 100 years of the
modern Monroe Doctrine, have created not only in Latin
America, and in the United States, but throughout the
world.

The only way to end all the misunderstanding and the
resentment aroused by this much-abused Monroe Doctrine,
and by the strange things which have been done in its
name, is to drop the Doctrine itself; and not to drop only
the modern versions of it—under which such things were
possible—but the original Doctrine as well, whence the misinterpretations and misuses sprang. No amount of explaining or repentance will suffice to restore confidence in the old
Doctrine, even if deprived of all the corollaries and mal-
formations added by Monroe's successors. Besides, we have
seen that even the merits of the original Monroe Doctrine
have been grossly exaggerated.

· · · · ·

With this in mind, let us outline, then, a three-point program. . . .

Point Number One: Abandonment of the
Monroe Doctrine

The necessity, and the urgency, of discarding the Monroe
Doctrine, worn-out, misunderstood, and distorted beyond
recognition, may be best emphasized by listing the ten

different counts of this *indictment* of the Doctrine which have been borne out in the preceding chapters.

1. The Monroe Doctrine was not intended for the benefit of the Latin-American republics.

2. The original results and merits of the Monroe Doctrine have been grossly exaggerated.

3. The Monroe Doctrine is worn-out and useless.

4. The Monroe Doctrine is a unilateral, egoistic policy, and exclusively of the United States.

5. The Monroe Doctrine did not create Pan-Americanism, but, on the contrary, it arrested the Bolivarian Pan-Americanism of equal rights and mutual obligations.

6. The Monroe Doctrine has been violated and disregarded by the European powers against which it was directed, with the knowledge and, at times, the connivance of the United States.

7. The Monroe Doctrine has been distorted to serve as an instrument of the hegemony of the United States in the Western Hemisphere.

8. The Monroe Doctrine has been misinterpreted and abused to serve as a cloak for the intervention of the United States in Latin America.

9. The Monroe Doctrine has been misconstrued and misused to serve as the tool of United States imperialism in the Caribbean area.

10. The Monroe Doctrine is in conflict with all the modern peace machinery of the world and the present trends of international relations.

Point Number Two: Substitution of a Pan-American Doctrine of Joint Responsibility

To take care of the problems of protection and joint action in case of anarchy, a Pan-American doctrine should be adopted by all the American states which would transfer the self-appointed powers until now held by the United States, alone, to a continental organization which would have in mind the rights of all, instead of the privilege of one.

Three steps can facilitate this:

A) Calling of a Pan-American conference, in which the chief problems involved in the political and economic relations of the United States with the Latin-American countries would be frankly discussed, the United States formally renouncing whatever privileges it has appropriated to itself under the Monroe Doctrine. It goes without saying that the kind of Pan-American conferences we have been having for the past forty years—which correspond faithfully to the kind of Pan-Americanism represented today by the *Pan American Union,* the Pan-Americanism of *recommendations,* diplomatic flirting, and bouquets of flowers—would not do at all.

. . . . .

B) Adoption by all the American states of the good principles involved in the original Monroe Doctrine, that is, the principles of opposition to non-American colonization of American territory and opposition to non-American interference with American governments for the purpose of oppressing or controlling them. This could be done jointly or separately, either by each American government issuing a declaration to that effect . . . or, better still, though greater obstacles inhere in this method, by signing a *continental pact of self-defense* in case of non-American aggression, just as Bolívar, the Liberator, planned. This would not be a mere internationalization or continentalization of the original Monroe Doctrine, as most of its advocates call it, both here and in Latin America, because, as we have seen, the original Monroe Doctrine was not advanced for the purpose of serving as a guarantee of mutual defense. It would really be an entirely new thing, establishing in a contractual form the guarantee which early Latin-American leaders thought, erroneously, the Monroe Doctrine gave them. It would, in fact, be more the enactment of the *Bolivarian doctrine* than the continentalization of the Monroe Doctrine. But it would serve better than anything else the only laudable principle which could have justified the Monroe Doctrine if the Doctrine had adhered strictly to it, and only to it, instead of refusing to sanction it for fear of foreign commitments and "entanglements," namely, the principle of *contractual continental self-defense.*

C) Devising and adopting, by all the American states, of a *Pan-American Doctrine of Joint Responsibility,* that is, one which would give all of them a voice in the solution of any controversies arising out of the problem of protection of foreign lives in any one of them where internal anarchy had completely destroyed any semblance of local government.

This doctrine would provide for the respect of the sovereignty and independence of the weakest as well as the strongest of the American republics, and for the consultation of all the American governments before any action, any *joint action* for purely humanitarian purposes, could be undertaken in any country where civil war had plunged the foreign, as well as the native population, into chaos and anarchy. This doctrine would proscribe hegemony and overlordship of any one of the nation members of the American family. It would proscribe the sort of intervention which we have witnessed in the past and which constitutes, today, the greatest barrier to Pan-American harmony. It would take the *big stick* out of the hands of Uncle Sam, who has certainly shown himself incapable of using it wisely, and it would place it in the hands of the *international community*, in this case, the American community of nations, the only one entitled to brandish it, to be used reluctantly and solely in extreme emergencies.

Point Number Three: Organization of American Peace

The logical complement of the steps suggested, and a necessary complement if the friendship and cooperation of the American republics are to be established on solid ground, should be the effective organization of international peace in the Western Hemisphere.

. . . . .

CANADA AND THE
MONROE DOCTRINE

Charles G. Fenwick

The relation of Canada to the Monroe Doctrine, particularly under the exigencies of World War II, was reviewed by Dr. Charles G. Fenwick (1880–   ) in the following editorial note in the *American Journal of International Law* in October 1938. Long a professor of international law at Bryn Mawr College, he was appointed a member of the United States delegation to the Inter-American Conference for the Maintenance of Peace at Buenos Aires in 1936 and to the eighth and ninth Inter-American Conferences in 1938 and 1948. In 1940 he became a member of the Inter-American Neutrality Committee, later the Inter-American Juridical Committee, and after 1948 director of the Department of International Law and Organization of the Pan American Union.

On August 18, [1938,] at Kingston, Ontario, President Roosevelt, upon receiving the honorary degree of Doctor of Laws

Charles G. Fenwick, "Canada and the Monroe Doctrine," *The American Journal of International Law*, XXXII (October 1938), 782–785.

from Queen's University, referred to the "common inheritance" of democratic ideals in Canada and the United States and to the "dangers from overseas" threatening that inheritance. Canada and the United States, as part of an international civilization, were resolved, he said, to leave no pathway unexplored which might contribute to the peace of the world; but if that hope were disappointed, they might assure each other "that this hemisphere at least shall remain a strong citadel wherein civilization can flourish unimpaired." Continuing, the President used these significant words:

> The Dominion of Canada is part of the sisterhood of the British Empire. I give to you assurance that the people of the United States will not stand idly by if domination of Canadian soil is threatened by any other empire.

For many years it has been assumed by publicists and statesmen that Canada was included within the scope of the Monroe Doctrine; but not until the President's address at Kingston had an explicit official statement been made to that effect. On November 27, 1936, on his way to the Conference at Buenos Aires, President Roosevelt had, as he expressed it at Kingston, "included Canada in the fellowship of the Americas"; but, inasmuch as Canada was not represented at the Conference, it meant no more than that Canada was part of a sort of mystical "family of American states." At Kingston, for the first time, Canada was formally promised the protection of the United States against an attack from any other source than the empire of which it is itself a part.

Did the President's statement amount to an "expansion" of the Monroe Doctrine? Was the assurance given to Canada more than a new application of an established policy? The question was raised by press correspondents within a few hours of the statement. In answer the President insisted that his words did not imply any enlargement or expansion of the Doctrine, and that he did not interpret the Doctrine as excluding Canada from the American states, colonies, and dependencies which the Doctrine sought to protect from foreign invasion or resettlement.

To raise a question as to the meaning and scope of the

Monroe Doctrine is to create an academic field-day for scholars. Forth come the precedents of the past and the new issue of Canada must be tested by them. If Canada cannot be brought under the original Monroe Doctrine, can it be fitted into any of the subsequent developments of the Doctrine? The issue is important only because the Monroe Doctrine has come to hold so sacred a place in the foreign policy of the United States that to maintain that it includes Canada is to end all public criticism of the wisdom of the President's statement; whereas if the promise made by the President to Canada is an extension of the Doctrine into a new field, then the promise may be debated upon its own merits without fear of touching the ark of the covenant.

That the Monroe Doctrine of today has far outgrown the precise terms in which it was formulated by President Monroe, no one would question. Monroe was confronted with a specific problem. The "Allied powers," as he described them, were threatening to give aid to Spain to restore her colonies to their former allegiance, just as they had given aid to Ferdinand of Spain to restore the monarchy. If this were done, and if the new governments of America, which had declared their independence of Spain and which had been recognized as independent by the United States, were to be suppressed, not only would the United States lose the benefit of the new commercial relations which had been established with those states, but it would find the armaments of the Allied powers at its very door. It was a matter of vital importance, therefore, for the United States that the Allied powers should be kept on their side of the ocean. It was not altruism, it was not sympathy with the struggle of the American states for their independence that dictated the Doctrine, although such sympathy, repeatedly appealed to in the orations of Henry Clay, played a large part in building up public opinion in support of the new policy. Rather it was the fundamental law of self-defense that lay at the basis of the Doctrine; and in that essential respect the Doctrine went back beyond the time of Monroe to Washington and Jefferson.

The actual terms in which the Monroe Doctrine was formulated were limited, therefore, to the situation to be met. At the time Monroe read his message, the Doctrine applied only to the American governments which had declared their independence and had been recognized as independent by the United States. Monroe expressly stated that "with the existing colonies or dependencies of any European power we have not interfered and shall not interfere." Even in respect to the governments that had been recognized, it was announced that the United States would remain neutral so long as it was a question of war between them and Spain. It was only when other European powers sought to "interpose" between Spain and her former colonies, either to oppress them or to control in any other manner their destiny, that the United States uttered a warning. In more general terms, any attempt on the part of the allied powers "to extend their system to any portion of this hemisphere" would be considered by the United States as "dangerous to our peace and safety."

But if the original Monroe Doctrine applied only to the American states whose independence the United States had up to that date recognized, the phrasing of the declaration was broad enough to permit it to cover the new states of America as one by one they declared their independence and were recognized as independent by the United States. When Brazil was recognized as independent in 1824, the Doctrine applied to it as much as if it had been recognized with Buenos Aires (Argentine Republic) and others during the months preceding the announcement of the Doctrine. When the Republic of Colombia divided itself into New Granada, Ecuador, and Venezuela, the Monroe Doctrine applied to all three separately as it had applied to them in unison. So also the Doctrine applied not only to the Federation of Central American States in 1824, but to the five separate members of the Federation when they became independent states a generation later.

But the Monroe Doctrine soon broadened beyond the original terms in which Monroe had formulated it. Two decades went by before it was put to a test, and by that time it was interpreted to mean that there must be no transfer of American territory from one European power to another, quite apart from the wishes of the inhabitants of the colony involved in the transfer. Moreover, no American state, to avoid domestic difficulties, might offer its sovereignty to a foreign power. Still later it was decided that no European power might assist one faction in an American state to maintain itself in power against the will of the majority of the population. By the close of the century the Monroe Doctrine was extended to ban the encroachment upon the territory of an American state by a European power possessing an adjacent colony. The opening of the twentieth century saw a prohibition of the occupation of the soil of an American state for the purpose of collecting debts. In 1912 a Senate resolution extended the Monroe Doctrine to include the lease by a private company of a harbor upon the western coast of Mexico when it appeared that the possession of the harbor by the company would give to Japan "practical power of control for national purposes." Asiatic powers were thus added to the earlier European powers. At the present day it may be said that the Monroe Doctrine extends to any attack by any non-American power upon an independent American state, and any attack upon a colony or dependency of a European power by a non-American power other than its sovereign. The terms of the Buenos Aires Convention for the Maintenance, Preservation and Reestablishment of Peace are broad—"in the event that the peace of the American republics is menaced . . . "—but they do not go beyond the existing scope of the Monroe Doctrine.

Does the fact that Canada is a member of the British Commonwealth of Nations and, as such, is within the larger group of the British Empire, preclude it from being brought within the terms of the Monroe Doctrine? Hitherto there has never been any suggestion but that the defense of the British Empire might safely be left to Great Britain. But there is little doubt that if at any time during the nineteenth century there had been question of the enforced transfer, say, of Jamaica to a stronger European power in consequence of a defeat of the British navy, the United States would have intervened to prevent the danger to its own peace and safety. The change of circumstances which now makes it necessary to consider the possibility that Great Britain, in the event of war in Europe or in the Far East, might not be able to assure the defense of Canada, is merely the occasion for the application to Canada of a policy long since developed to meet similar situations.

What is novel in the case of Canada is the fact that while Canada, since the Statute of Westminster of 1931, is practically an independent sovereign state, yet it is, under the forms of law, a part of the British Empire and is, moreover, bound to the Empire by very strong ties of sentiment. Neither of these considerations would seem, however, to bear upon the question at issue. All of the Latin-American republics have been at one time or another members of the League of Nations and, as such, under obligation to regard a resort to war against one member of the League as an act of war committed against themselves, with the resulting obligation of severing all trade and financial relations with the covenant-breaking state. Yet the United States, while modifying its neutrality legislation to take account of Latin-American states's being engaged in war with a non-American state when cooperating with the League of Nations, has never regarded such a situation as modifying in any degree the necessity of preventing European or Asiatic encroachment upon the same American states. For the Monroe Doctrine, it must be remembered, is a doctrine of long-range self-defense. Not so long-range as if it sought to prevent aggression in any part of the world, but clear and definite as to aggression against the states of America. Even the fact that the American state may have been to some degree responsible for creating the conditions that led to the aggression against it has not altered the determination of the United States to keep any nations that might seek to play the part of the original "Allied powers" from extending their system to any portion of this hemisphere.

It would seem that the formal application to Canada of the policy of the Monroe Doctrine should properly lead to the formal inclusion of Canada in the circle of "American republics" and to participation by Canada in the coming Eighth International Conference of American States at Lima. Elsewhere the writer has expressed the view that Canada as a member of the International American Conferences would not only add to the list of states which are carrying on the traditions of democratic government believed by the United States to be essential to peace, but might be expected to take a constructive part in the development of new principles of law to meet the changing conditions of American life.

A JAPANESE VIEW

Katsuji Inahara

The Monroe Doctrine viewed as a principle of United
States hegemony over the Western Hemisphere was
used by the Axis Powers, Japan and Germany, as justification for their imperialistic objectives respectively
in Asia and Europe. The parallelism between the Monroe Doctrine of the United States and Japan's Greater
East Asia Co-Prosperity Sphere was effectively demonstrated in 1940 by Katsuji Inahara, the editor of
Contemporary Japan, a political and economic monthly
review published in Tokyo.

War is mischievous, for it occasionally produces wholly unexpected results or by-products. Recent discussion of the
Monroe Doctrine resulting in the conclusion that it has
been brought up to date, or at least is in the process of
being brought up to date, is a case in point. The attitude of
the United States toward the present war in Europe has
been characterized by the American slogan "safeguarding
democracy," but this slogan can hardly be an abstract assertion of an objective nature. It certainly must have as its
basis or background practical considerations of a subjective

Katsuji Inahara, "An Asiatic Views a U.S. Doctrine," *Living Age,*
CCCLIX (November 1940), 256–262.

nature for the safeguarding of the United States itself. To be exact, the term "safeguarding democracy" has been conceived with the idea that Great Britain and France constitute a bulwark against the menace of totalitarianism, and, therefore, to protect this bulwark is to defend the United States itself.

Then what is the real meaning of protecting the United States? It cannot, for one thing, be other than safeguarding the Monroe Doctrine. The upshot so far of the European war in which the United States is economically participating for the specific purpose of defending the Monroe Doctrine, however, has placed it upon the table of international analytical operation and has thus afforded a chance for its reconsideration. Such a turn of events was evidently never expected either by the United States or by the rest of the world. This is where the mischievous nature of war comes in.

Discussion concerning the Monroe Doctrine started in earnest on June 18, [1940,] when the American Congress adopted a resolution stating that "the United States will not recognize any transfer or cession of territorial possessions of a non-American power in the Western Hemisphere to any other non-American power." In due course of time the belligerent powers, especially Germany and Italy, were notified of this resolution. Since the capitulation of Paris to the Germans took place on June 13 and France's surrender four days later, there is no room for doubt that this resolution was passed under the influence of such reverses in the European situation. The purpose of the resolution was to reiterate the traditional policy of the United States and uphold the Monroe Doctrine.

The formal adoption of the resolution and its notification to the powers concerned immediately invited opposition from Berlin, a development which the United States had not, in all probability, expected. On July 1, Berlin sent an official note to Washington to the following effect:

> The German Minister for Foreign Affairs states that Germany is unable to perceive for what reason the United States government has addressed the note to Germany. He states that in contrast with other countries, especially in contrast with Britain and France, Germany has no territorial possessions on the American continent and has given no occasion whatever for the

assumption that it intends to acquire such possessions, and asserts that thus, insofar as Germany is concerned, the communication addressed to Germany is without object.

In case the interpretation of the Monroe Doctrine is implicit in the United States government's communication, it amounts to conferring upon some European countries the right to possess territories in the Western Hemisphere but denies it to other European countries. It is obvious that such an interpretation would be untenable.

The German note was evidently a telling thrust at the very point of inconsistency in the American attitude, suggesting as it did the unlikelihood that the Monroe Doctrine, as interpreted by the United States, would be accepted by the world in general. The case is exactly similar to the inconsistency shown by the United States in asserting the Monroe Doctrine on the one hand, while seeking to maintain the principle of the Open Door on the other. The world would find it difficult to accept such mutually incompatible claims. In reply to the German objection, the United States declared through a statement issued by Secretary of State Cordell Hull that "the Monroe Doctrine rests solely on a policy of self-defense, and it contains within it not the slightest vestige or implication, much less any assumption of hegemony on the part of the United States."

But the obvious impression gained from such a declaration is that it falls far short of refuting effectively the assertion of the German government, for the crucial points raised by the latter are that:

1. Why does the United States now oppose the acquisition of territories in the Western Hemisphere by some countries of Europe, while it has no objection to other European powers having territorial possessions there?

2. If the United States can rightfully exclude European intervention in the American continents, there is no reason why one of the European countries cannot demand nonintervention of the United States in Europe. Is it not inconsistent for the United States to intervene in Europe and at the same time to object to European intervention in the Americas?

And on these crucial points Secretary Hull made only an

evasive answer without directly replying to the points raised. Thus arguments on the question of the Monroe Doctrine resulted in giving the impression to the world at large that Germany was the winner, theoretically at least.

Moreover, the Hull statement cannot be considered to be wholly without doubtful points. Nothing, for instance, was said exactly which would afford a standard of judging whether the Monroe Doctrine can be justified or refuted on the basis of the question of "establishment of hegemony." The United States may have its own idea regarding the meaning of hegemony, but it is by no means thoroughly understood by other countries.

By hegemony Secretary Hull may mean control by force of arms. But such an idea is obsolete. It is true that a superior armed force can bring other countries under its control, but it is not by armed force alone that such control is acquired. It is easily possible to subjugate other peoples by economic strength, for economic methods when applied with hostile intent are fully as murderous as military force. That the United States has revised its neutrality law for the purpose of extending economic assistance to Great Britain and France can be understood only in the light of this truism. The abrogation of the Commercial Treaty with Japan also may become sufficiently clear as to its real purpose when viewed from this standpoint. In our opinion, hegemony is not established through the might of arms alone, and therefore, it seems neither fair nor compatible with modern thought to proscribe hegemony as control by armed force and try to exclude it. To speak plainly, even the United States, professing as it does its opposition to the establishment of hegemony by arms, proposed at the Pan-American conference held at Lima in 1938, the formation of a sort of military alliance among the countries of the American continents with the American navy as its propelling force under the assumption that "the countries of American continents will take defensive measures against invasion from outside countries, regarding them as their common enemy." Such an attitude on the part of the United States clearly testifies to the fact that that country does not necessarily entertain such a Puritan idea as to exclude, when advantageous to itself, all intention of employing methods of military control.

While the United States was not a little chagrined at the German challenge for a rational definition of the Monroe Doctrine, Foreign Minister Hachiro Arita of Japan, in his radio speech on June 29, said the following:

> Since it is difficult to realize peace throughout the world in the present stage of human progress, peoples who are closely related to one another geographically, culturally, and economically should establish a regional sphere of their own for their common existence and prosperity and establish therein peace and order as the first step toward world-wide peace. East Asia and the region of the South Seas should in this sense come under the same sphere.

What Foreign Minister Arita said by no means contained any novel idea; it was merely a reiteration of the substance of what has on many occasions in the past been stated by Japanese statesmen and diplomats. Nobody in Japan thought that the speech was of such a character as to become a subject of heated discussion. Strange to say, however, it aroused widespread repercussions in other countries, especially in the United States. At a press interview on July 5, Secretary of State Cordell Hull expressed his disapproval of the Japanese policy as enunciated by Mr. Arita in his radio speech or what the United States thought that speech expressed. Mr. Hull said:

> It [the Monroe Doctrine] never resembled and it doesn't today resemble policies which appear to be arising in other geographical areas of the world which are alleged to be similar to the Monroe Doctrine, but which, instead of resting solely on policies of self-defense and respect for existing sovereign rights, as does the Monroe Doctrine, would seem to be only a pretext for carrying out the conquest by sword, military occupation, and complete economic and political domination by certain powers of other free independent peoples.

What Mr. Arita asserted, however, was that there is in the present world a rampant economic exclusionism, trade barriers, and racial discrimination which are constantly producing causes of war; that since it is impossible to secure world peace in the existing situation by eliminating such causes of war, the only practical method to achieve the purpose of peace would be for the peoples who are so situated geographically, economically, and otherwise as to be able to carry on a cooperative life to form a sphere of their own, minister to the needs of one another, and thus enjoy peace and prosperity; that the realization of such a regional peace would in itself be a contribution toward world peace; and that since East Asia and the South Seas are a region having such common requisites, it would be well for them to form a sphere for their common existence and prosperity. Such being the plan suggested by Foreign Minister Arita, it contains no loophole through which an idea of aggression, acquisition of rights and interests, or territorial encroachment, as might have been erroneously suspected by Mr. Hull, can enter.

If East Asia and the South Seas become a unit of existence with organic systems and structures, it naturally will assure the firm establishment of the principle of self-defense as suggested by Mr. Hull as being the objective of the Monroe Doctrine. It will, moreover, serve to substantiate in a practical manner respect for the sovereignty of each nation. The reason for this is the fact that it is totally unthinkable that nations who want to safeguard jointly their common interests under the principle of common existence and common prosperity should engage in controversies or refuse to cooperate for their own defense.

Viewed from this standpoint, the Monroe Doctrine, as defined by Secretary of State Hull, and Japan's policy, as expressed in the Arita speech, are not necessarily incompatible with each other. The world has been under the impression that the Monroe Doctrine as practised by the United States in Latin America and that as defined by Mr. Hull are not by any means one and the same. Although Secretary Hull's definition of the Monroe Doctrine and Japanese policy differ from each other in their starting point, they are not so divergent in their ultimate purpose as Mr. Hull seems to have tried to impress upon the world through his statement. Since the Monroe Doctrine originated in the desire to exclude European intervention in the Americas, though from the standpoint of self-defense, its spirit is one of exclusionism. Japan's policy with regard to

East Asia and the South Seas, on the other hand, is to convert this part of the world into an experimental laboratory, so to speak, for the establishment of peace to come after the present war, and there realize an economic stability which is an essential basis of peace. Therefore, the two policies are completely different from each other at their starting point. However, there are some people in other countries, especially in the United States, who consider the suggestion of Mr. Arita as an East Asiatic "Monroe Doctrine." Such an appellation is simply a misnomer in the light of the above circumstances. But the American Monroe Doctrine and the regional system as advocated by Japan are not by any means so irreconcilably different from each other in their ultimate purpose and especially in the outward form.

．　．　．　．　．

THE MONROE DOCTRINE
IN WORLD WAR II

Dexter Perkins

Dexter Perkins (1889–   ), professor emeritus of history at the University of Rochester, has built his academic career on his studies of the Monroe Doctrine, starting with *The Monroe Doctrine, 1823–1826* (1927), and continuing with *The Monroe Doctrine, 1826–1867* (1933), *The Monroe Doctrine, 1867–1907* (1937), and *Hands Off: The History of the Monroe Doctrine* (1941), later reissued as *A History of the Monroe Doctrine* (1955). In the following article, published in 1941, he applied the principles of the Monroe Doctrine to the situation presented to the United States by the threat of the Axis Powers.

. . . . .

Perhaps the nearest approach to national unity in the field of foreign affairs has to do with the Monroe Doctrine. There is significance in the recent unanimous vote of both Houses

Dexter Perkins, "The Monroe Doctrine Today," *Yale Review*, XXX (June 1941), 686–702. Reprinted by permission of Yale University Press.

of Congress reaffirming one of its most important principles. Few decisions of the present administration have awakened more universal commendation than the extension of Monroe's principles to the island of Greenland. It is probable that most Americans, if asked if they believed in the Monroe Doctrine, would respond with a ringing affirmative.

There are, however, many points about President Monroe's message of 1823 which need clarification in these days of international tension. And if, as seems probable, the Doctrine is going to play a still larger role in public discussion, it seems essential that it should be accurately understood.

. . . . . .

And now let us turn to the present. First of all, in the great debate between isolationists and advocates of aid to Britain, what have we to learn from the declaration of 1823? Superficially, the case may seem stronger for the isolationists. Monroe's message seems to draw a sharp line between the New World and the Old. It emphasizes the cleavage of the continents.

But there is, it might well be maintained, another side to the matter. The message of 1823 was one of the great pronunciamentos of the nineteenth century in the cause of free government as against despotism. It was a paean of praise of the democratic system. It drew a line of cleavage not only between geographical areas but between political systems, between republicanism and despotism.

Viewed from this angle, then, in the struggle of two ideological systems, the Monroe Doctrine wears an aspect not so pleasing to the friends of isolation. In 1823 it might be true that the ideal set forth in the message was almost exclusively an American ideal. One hundred and eighteen years ago, there was not a republican government in Europe save Switzerland, and Switzerland was ruled by an oligarchy. Great Britain had not yet undergone even the first of those peaceful revolutions in the working out of the democratic process that was to take shape in the Reform Bill of 1832. In France, the government of the *Charte* was a government of a restricted group, reactionary in form and spirit. Russia, Austria, and Prussia were still more autocratically ruled. Europe *did* stand in opposition to America then, certainly in opposition to the United States; and European Continental statesmen viewed the democratic aspirations of the Americans with distaste, and sometimes with disgust. There *was* a line of division then between the New World and the Old in the sphere of political forms.

Today many persons would maintain that such a line cannot be drawn with any degree of clarity. When we survey the institutions of the great states of the world, when we try their professions by their deeds, when we seek to weigh their loyalty to the democratic faith by their habits, their broad tolerances, their respect for the dignity of the individual man, we look first of all in kinship and in admiration to the people of Great Britain. It is they who illustrate the power of the democratic ideal; imperfectly, of course, as inheres in the weakness of human nature; but none the less more strikingly and more heroically than any other people in the world. Can it be thought that in the field of ideas the future of the inhabitants of the British Commonwealth of Nations has no relevance? Can it be thought, for the matter of that, that the strengthening of the democratic ideal in the states of Latin America will be unaffected by the events now taking place in the mists of the Channel, in the perilous reaches of the North Atlantic, in the shattered cities and devastated countryside of Britain? If the message of 1823 be taken as a call to the defense of a political ideal, then its spirit today does not call for aloofness so much as for assistance to the great democracy across the seas.

It is going too far, however, to assert that the events of 1823 furnish a convincing precedent for common action with Great Britain. The negotiations preceding the enunciation of the Doctrine did not result in any concert of action between the United States and Great Britain for the defense of the New World against the tyrants of Continental Europe. There was, it is true, talk of such a concert. When Monroe received the correspondence of Richard Rush, he sent it to the venerable Jefferson and to the aging Madison. Both these men advised close cooperation with the British government, and the President himself in a measure inclined to the same course. But John Quincy Adams would have none of it. He suspected the purposes of Canning, and he took the position that it would be "more dignified to avow our principles explicitly to Great Britain [*sic*, Russia] and France than to come in as a cock-boat in the wake of the British man-of-war." His views prevailed; and the message of 1823, far from being a matter of concert with Great Britain, was, rather, an effort to anticipate her action, and to gain credit by so doing.

Moreover, the friends of assistance to Britain err, in my judgment, when they proffer the generalization, as they sometimes do, that during the nineteenth century and the first decade of the twentieth century, the British fleet protected the New World from peril, and thus enforced the Monroe Doctrine. The plain fact of the matter is that during this happy period, there were few actual threats, and certainly few serious threats to the integrity of the American republics.

The peril to the new states in 1823 has now been shown to be illusory, completely illusory. In the years from 1823 to 1860, such issues as involved the Doctrine were very largely issues with Great Britain herself—the question of the Falkland Islands, the consolidation of British sovereignty in Belize, the seizure of the Bay Islands off the coast of Honduras, the question of the Mosquito Coast. During the Civil War, it is true, the France of Louis Napoleon, long jealous of the influence of the United States in Mexico, threw off the mask and installed a puppet Emperor, the Austrian Archduke Maximilian, in the castle of Chapultepec. But the British, while they discouraged, certainly did not oppose, this venture; and the enterprise itself collapsed for reasons which had nothing to do with the attitude of London, but much to do with the attitude of Washington. The French intervention in Mexico once over, there followed a long period in which no ambitious projects against the Latin-American republics were even formulated; Great Britain gravitated towards a more cordial relationship with the United States; France was busy building up her colonial domain in Africa and the Far East; German naval power was not yet born. Down to the end of the nineteenth century, therefore, the New World was in no danger from the territorial ambition of the Old; and here again, as in the earlier period, the most serious difference of opinion with regard to the Monroe Doctrine was with Great Britain—when the Cleveland administration demanded the arbitration of Britain's boundary controversy with Venezuela over British Guiana.

As the German people aroused themselves to dreams of

larger power with the turn of the century, and began to challenge the naval power of Britain, their naval leaders undoubtedly cast their eyes on bases in the New World; but their Foreign Office remained cautious and conservative; and despite the legend that Theodore Roosevelt prevented a German occupation of Venezuelan harbors, there is no evidence in German or other archives that nefarious enterprises were afoot. The morals of the present German government make it easy to believe the worst of Germans in this or any other epoch; but the facts of the past, so far as we know them, do not justify the thesis that the New World was saved from some ambitious enterprise of imperialism by the might of Great Britain.

To say this is not to say, of course, that the destruction of British naval power, and the defeat of Great Britain, in this present war would be without effect upon the evolution of the Monroe Doctrine. For during a period of more than 100 years, during most of which she has been the greatest naval power in the world, Great Britain has used that power, so far as the Western Hemisphere is concerned, with a moderation which deserves recognition. At a time when in material resources and naval force she was infinitely superior to any other state, she took almost no steps to enlarge her territorial possessions in the New World, or to impose her system upon any New World state. Would a completely triumphant Germany practise a similar moderation?

. . . . . .

If, therefore, we wish to avoid the challenge to democracy in the New World, we must sustain democracy in the Old. Looking at the matter from this angle of vision, the assistance which has recently been pledged to Great Britain is a kind of insurance for the preservation of the principles of 1823.

Such assistance, of course, is not so regarded by Herr von Ribbentrop, or by the German press. From Berlin, from the Foreign Minister himself, indeed, has come a very different interpretation of the Monroe Doctrine. If the United States expects to be free from all interference in this hemisphere, runs this interpretation, then it must scrupulously refrain from all interference in the affairs of Europe. It is not necessary to comment on the effrontery of this proposal coming from the representative of a government which has never practised noninterference anywhere, and to which intrigue and the fomenting of internal strife are a natural stock in trade. It should merely be said that such an interpretation of the Monroe Doctrine is certainly not accepted by the people of the United States. Nor is it necessary that it should be. The American people have long believed that the New World should be secure from the aggression of the Old. But they have not on this account forsworn the right to protect their interests wherever those interests lie. Because they have a paramount interest in what happens, let us say, in the Caribbean, it does not follow that they have no interest whatever in what happens in the Orient or in Europe. The Monroe Doctrine is not a self-denying ordinance directed against all American diplomatic activity in the larger part of the world. It was hardly ever appealed to in the historic debates that preceded our entry into the World War in 1917. In the debates in the Senate of the United States on the Lease-Lend bill, it played no important part. The discrediting of National Socialism through the defeat of Hitler surely has something to do with the preservation in the New World of those democratic values to which the fifth President of the United States attached so much importance 118 years ago.

But the preservation of these values depends upon something more than the defeat of Germany. It depends upon the creation of cordial relations with the republics of the West. That task is one which has made great headway during the last fourteen years, and which is still in train.

Paradoxically enough, the most serious obstacle to close relations with the states to the south has undoubtedly lain in the turn given to the Monroe Doctrine by President Theodore Roosevelt and his immediate successors. Under this interpretation the United States, in order to prevent the intervention of European powers in the affairs of the New World, might be justified in taking police measures of its own in the more unruly of the republics. It might be justified, as a preventive measure, in assuming some measure of control over their finances. On the basis of these propositions (though, of course, not wholly owing to them), came the assumption of control of the customs of the Dominican Republic in 1905, the intervention in Nicaragua in 1912, the military occupation of Haiti in 1914, the complete extinction of the Dominican government and the establishment of military rule over the Dominican Republic in 1916. At the end of the great war for freedom and democracy, indeed, American marines had been installed upon the soil of no less than three Latin-American states.

But the American people have never cared very much for these policies of control. Their instinct for domination has often been counterbalanced by their faith in democracy, by their dislike of violence and of force where violence and force can be avoided. There were signs of reaction against the coercive policies of Theodore Roosevelt and Wilson in the administration of Secretary Hughes; there developed a fixed policy, the policy of the Good Neighbor, with Secretary Stimson and Secretary Hull. The American troops were withdrawn from the Dominican Republic in 1924; they were withdrawn from Nicaragua in 1929; they were withdrawn from Haiti in 1934. In the meantime, the Theodore Roosevelt "Corollary" to the Monroe Doctrine, as the interventionist interpretation of the Doctrine had come to be called, was gradually whittled down. In 1929, when the Senate of the United States ratified the Kellogg Pact (that melancholy monument to a bygone age), it did so with a kind of gloss which, amongst other things, analyzed the principles of 1823, and rejected the Theodore Roosevelt maxims; in 1930 the State Department published the so-called "Clark Memorandum" on the Doctrine, which adopted the same position. More important decisions were to come. The action of the Senate and that of the State Department were, after all, no more than non-binding expressions of intention; in 1933 came the Montevideo Conference, and at this conference Secretary Hull put his name to a convention which adopted the principle of nonintervention as a guiding principle of action in the relations of the American states. A still more definite expression of the same point of view was to be set forth in the convention of Buenos Aires in 1936. By solemn international agreement, the United States put behind it the policies of domination, and pledged itself to policies of abstention. And its decision in this regard, made by the Executive, was ratified, wonderful to relate, by the unanimous vote of the members of the United States Senate.

It is sometimes said by Japanese and by German propagandists, and even by representatives of their Foreign Offices, that their governments are now merely propounding a Monroe Doctrine for Asia, or a Monroe Doctrine for Europe. The comparison is an insolent one. For even at the most unfavorable interpretation, the United States has never used the principles of 1823 to justify aught more than a temporary, and an avowedly temporary, intervention. The maxims of Monroe have never been the basis of a ruthless and ambitious imperialism. There is nothing in American foreign policy today (and we can say it proudly) that justifies any comparison with Germany or with Japan.

The other peoples of the New World are not today quaking before ruthless military power exerted by the United States, as the few free peoples left in Europe must quake before Germany; no conquering armies suppress the liberties of nations, or plunder them of their resources, on this side of the Atlantic; no reign of violence overturns the temple of law, and makes havoc of civilization itself. To use the name of Monroe to justify what is now taking place in Europe and in Asia is indeed a grave perversion of history.

But the United States has done more in these last twelve years than free its foreign policy of the incubus of the Theodore Roosevelt Corollary, and win, more than ever before, the good will of the nations to the south; it has been forging a cooperative policy, a policy of hemispheric solidarity. This policy has been patiently pursued; it involves, in some degree, the internationalization of the Monroe Doctrine. At Buenos Aires, for example, in 1936, there was drawn up a consultative pact, binding the nations of the New World to take counsel among themselves in the case of peril from across the seas; and this pact, imperfect in form, was given a more precise character at the conference at Lima in December, 1938. At the same time, the twenty-one republics of this hemisphere joined together in an impressive declaration of fundamental principles which ought to govern the conduct and which ought to express the ideals of democratic states. Since then, cooperation has gone further; and its most impressive expression, from the standpoint of the student of the Monroe Doctrine, is the Declaration of Havana, of July 1940, by which there was worked out a common policy with relation to what has been called the "no-transfer" principle.

How far the movement adumbrated above will go, it is impossible to foresee. We cannot speak accurately of the complete internationalization of the Monroe Doctrine today; nothing less than a Pan-American alliance would be necessary to justify such a phrase—and nothing less than a common pledge to maintain the institutions of democracy, to boot. But we can say that progress has been made towards broadening the basis of the Doctrine; and we can say that American diplomacy has done much to give to the nations of the New World in this great hour of history a sense of common interest and of common destiny.

The task is an enormous one; the obstacles to its full accomplishment, in the economic, in the political, in the psychological field, are many; but there are few who will doubt that one of the major objectives of American foreign policy today lies in the tenacious pursuit of the Good Neighbor Policy, in closer economic relations with the states of the New World, in the preservation of their independence and the encouragement of their democratic aspirations.

Less than four years ago, on his return from Europe, Senator Key Pittman, then chairman of the Senate Committee on Foreign Relations, in a public interview, declared that the Monroe Doctrine was dead, that there was no more need for it. But this eminent authority has been proved wrong; wrong not in theory, but in the court of public opinion, and before the august tribunal of history itself. The Monroe Doctrine is not dead; it is not obsolete; it lives today, not merely in textbooks or academic discussion, but in the minds of the American people. For once again, perhaps more widely than in 1823, men believe the New World to be threatened by the ambition of the Old; we may think them right or wrong, or partly right and partly wrong; but we cannot deny the fact that most Americans, even if they do not believe that this hemisphere is in danger of physical assault, believe that its ideals, its way of life, are imperilled by the forces of National Socialism.

So believing, they are ready to gird themselves against the danger; so believing, they muster the mighty energies of this nation in a program of aid to Britain. In their present course of action, the doctrines enunciated by Monroe play a part, and that no small one; and the words which he wrote in 1823 come alive again in 1941.

ECONOMIC MONROEISM

Carlos Saavedra Lamas

The economic implications of modern Monroeism, as represented by the Good Neighbor Policy of the Franklin D. Roosevelt administration, were suggested by the president of the National University of Buenos Aires, Dr. Carlos Saavedra Lamas (1878–1959), in the following article. As Argentine Minister of Foreign Affairs from 1932 to 1938, Dr. Saavedra Lamas represented Argentina at the Seventh Inter-American Conference at Montevideo in 1933, at the Inter-American Conference for the Maintenance of Peace at Buenos Aires in 1936, and at other international meetings. He was awarded the Nobel Peace Prize in 1936.

The recent declaration [the Atlantic Charter] signed by the English and American statesmen cannot be anything but gratifying to Argentine sentiment and public opinion.

Its three principles coincide with the international principles of our country and have been followed consistently in our tradition.

. . . . .

The opposition to the right of conquest, which is set forth in the initial part of the declaration of Roosevelt and Chur-

Carlos Saavedra Lamas, "Monroísmo Económico," *Desfile*, Buenos Aires, September 17, 1941. Translated by the editor.

chill, has been assured in this continent from the First Inter-American Conference, meeting in Washington in 1889, which established that that principle was eliminated from American public law and refuses to recognize cessions of territory which are made under the threat of war or the pressure of violence.

It exemplifies, then, a new understanding with the great and noble American nation, paladin of justice in this convulsed world. Our effort ought to be directed toward arriving at an understanding also in economic matters of the highest importance for the aggrandizement of the whole continent.

We ought to ask the United States to contribute also to that pressing task. Mr. [Cordell] Hull has been the father or initiator of the ideas of liberal policy throughout the continent, which must not stop but must on the contrary grow and be put into practice in actual situations. President Roosevelt recalled in an address the concept of [Juan Bautista] Alberdi as to the continental unity and the political system which requires "the contribution of all for one and one for all." We must apply it to the economic order, to the strengthening and progress of all the sister republics of the continent, as we have accepted it in other orders.

The Monroe Doctrine has just been generalized for the whole continent. Not many years ago an Argentine delegate declared, in the name of his government, before the assembly in Geneva that the Argentine republic would not recognize the Doctrine as "a regional agreement." When the [Argentine] Congress approved the ratification of the treaty of the League of Nations, it made an express reservation of the Monroe Doctrine on the initiative of the Congress itself. The so-called Americanization of the Monroe Doctrine, proposed in the Pan-American Conference of Buenos Aires in 1910 and in the Conference of Jurists at Rio de Janeiro in 1927, has not yet been accepted. It remains only an expression of unilateral policy by the United States, as it has been proclaimed by its principal statesmen and great Presidents.

. . . . .

The expansion of the theory of Monroe, signalized in the last conference at Havana, in which the American nations agreed to join the United States in its opposition to the transfer of sovereignty to a non-American country, has been happily accepted by the Argentine delegate who attended that conference as a treaty *ad referendum,* subject to the approval of Congress, which has just been given.

In all respects this constitutes an amplification of the classic concept of Monroeism and a great extension of it to geographical regions to which we have not previously applied it, nor has the United States pretended to generalize it. It is certain that not until now has Argentina accepted the continental character of the Doctrine.

But if such should occur, it must be acknowledged that it is necessary also to give an economic significance to Monroeism.

The best guaranty of autonomy in law and of full sovereignty is in the increase of production, in internal progress, with its corresponding aggrandizement. Legal autonomy then will become autonomy in fact. Economic Monroeism ought to strengthen, raise, and consolidate the economic progress of all America.

And if all this transition, unexpressed but real, from many of the orientations which until now have been fundamental to Pan-Americanism, has been created by motives of defense in the face of the threats which it is alleged are suspended over the American continent, it is a fact that military defense is not adequate for frail and weak nations which lack economic power and actual force. Real defense requires also the economic strengthening of all the American republics since modern war depends on material skill, economic power, industrial force, and effective strength in those nations which become involved in it.

. . . . .

A LATIN AMERICAN
SPEAKS:
U.S. AGAINST US

Luis Quintanilla

Among the modern Latin-American critics of the Monroe Doctrine one of the most temperate is the Mexican
diplomat and author Luis Quintanilla (1900–   ).
He has represented his country in Rio de Janeiro,
Washington, Paris, and Moscow. In the following
chapter from his book *A Latin American Speaks* he
argues that the Doctrine should be supplanted by
"authentic, genuine Pan-Americanism."

At the time of its enunciation, the Monroe Doctrine was
intended to be, essentially, a policy toward Europe; not a
policy for the hemisphere. It was a toothless warning indeed, but one definitely aimed at Europe. As such, there is
nothing that we can hold against it. To reject its original
intention would be tantamount to accepting the right of
Europe to meddle with the nations of our hemisphere: and
that, no Latin American wants.

It is only by virtue of later interpretations—or rather

Luis Quintanilla, *A Latin American Speaks* (New York: Macmillan,
1943), pp. 111–130.

"misinterpretations"—that the momentous message was gradually fashioned into a Machiavellian policy for *intra*-hemisphere consumption. From a candid but commendable United States gesture against European interference, the Doctrine was turned into a ruthless axiom, utilized by Washington administrations to suit the interests of what is known as *Yankee Imperialism*. Because the Doctrine—certainly through no fault of its victims—was perverted to the point of being invoked as a justification for attacks against the sovereignty of the nations which it claimed to protect, it bulks large today as a stumbling block in the way of inter-American relations. "Paramount Interests," "Manifest Destiny," "Big-Stick Policy," "Watchful Waiting," "Dollar Diplomacy," "Paternalism," "Protectionism"—in short, "Yankee Imperialism"—those slogans have become irrevocably connected, in the minds of Latin Americans, with the two words, *Monroe Doctrine*.

Yes, it may be said that historically there are *two* Monroe Doctrines: the one, promulgated by the President; and the other, the distorted Doctrine of the Corollaries. But the authentic one has been pushed into the background. Today people have not in mind the mild offering of the fifth President of the United States, but the subsequent concoction into which entered all the imperialistic ingredients added by more voracious occupants of the White House, among whom Theodore Roosevelt—twenty-sixth President of the United States of America—stands out conspicuously.

• • • • •

Practically any Spanish American could put forward an impressive list of perfectly legitimate reasons why he rejects vehemently the Monroe Doctrine. A striking sample of genuine Latin-American attitude in this respect can be found in Gaston Nerval's book, significantly entitled *Autopsy of the Monroe Doctrine*.

"Autopsy" is perhaps wishful thinking. The *original* Doctrine is not dead. The Axis has given it a shot in the arm. To handle the *original* Doctrine as if it were dead would be not "autopsy" but vivisection. It is not dead, yet the weight of its additions places it beyond redemption. The Corollaries have become an intrinsic part of it. We cannot and must not forget them. No historical or diplomatic surgeon could sever the Doctrine from the acts of aggression committed in its name; not even Professor Perkins, family doctor of Monroe's troublesome child, nor official interpreter Reuben Clark and his authoritative *Memorandum*. After all, a political doctrine should not be judged by its intent only, but also by its results. Scores of charges can be leveled at the Monroe Doctrine by a Latin American. For the sake of clearness, I will limit the counts of my indictment to five:

1) It is *unilateral*.
2) It proved *inefficient*.
3) It was *perverted*.
4) It is *unpopular*.
5) It has become *outmoded*.

1) There can be no argument concerning the first count. Practically all historians, Anglo-Saxon as well as Latin, agree on that. Even Dr. Perkins writes: "The Monroe Doctrine was not, and was not intended to be, anything else than a unilateral declaration of policy. From that day to this American statesmen have insisted upon its purely American character, upon the right of the United States to interpret it in its own fashion, and on the basis of its own interests."

. . . . .

There is nothing the matter with a *unilateral* policy. But its interpreters have no right to make it multilateral. The Monroe Doctrine was never meant to be anything but a one-sided policy. To pretend otherwise, is to commit historical heresy. It is not saving the Monroe Doctrine but rather confessing, by implication, that it has ceased to exist.

The Doctrine was a *monologue,* not a dialogue. It assumed, after the Theodore Roosevelt Corollary, an order of things entirely created and maintained by a self-appointed *guardian;* not one agreed to by equal partners. Why speak of "Americanization" or "continentalization"? Whatever rabbits Monroeist magicians pull out of their hats, that thing called Pan-Americanism will never come out of it!

The Doctrine was unilateral not only in its proclamation, definition, and application, but also in its original motive, which was not the safety of the hemisphere, but the security of the United States. . . . The security of the United States: again, there is nothing the matter with that. Pan-Americanism also includes it—but does not stop there. It cares not only for the security of the United States but for that of all and each of the American republics. *Good-Neighbor Pan-Americanism is a joint enterprise freely undertaken by part-*

ners with equal rights and mutual obligations. And that is precisely what the Monroe Doctrine is not!

2) *The Doctrine proved inefficient.* To be accurate, one should say that it was created impotent. It was the expression of a wish: to remove from the Western Hemisphere the threat of European military or political interference. But there was never mention of specific measures to be taken, should that wish go unheeded. Every North American statesman made it clear that the Doctrine never implied the slightest pledge by the United States actually to fight for the sovereignty of any American republic. The man who as Secretary of State is credited with the drafting of the message read by President Monroe to Congress—John Quincy Adams—said in a message to the Senate December 26, 1825, after he had become President of his country: "An agreement between all the parties represented at the meeting that each will guard *by its own means* against the establishment of any future European colony within its border may be found advisable. This was more than two years since announced by my predecessor." It could not be clearer: *"each . . . by its own means."* From the outset and from the lips of the statesmen who played the principal parts in the elaboration of the Doctrine, the world was advised that it was up to every country by its own means to uphold Monroe's recommendation, with the inference that, should any European nation violate such recommendation, the United States would not consider itself obligated to act; nor, of course, the other American republics. The Monroe Doctrine was too platonic to be effective. . . . When there is no sanction, any transgressor is willing to take the risk. To consider European infringements as "the manifestation of an unfriendly disposition toward the United States" was not enough. Monroe did not say "act of hostility" but simply "unfriendly disposition." Little wonder that European interventions, of all kinds, took place from 1823 on.

The Doctrine was appealed to in vain by some Latin-American countries because of optimistic misinterpretations (improving the essence of the message, not perverting it). The Doctrine did not bind the United States to any joint resistance against Europe. It never placed upon the United States the heavy burden of protecting the hemisphere. The Corollaries of the Doctrine tended in that direction, but Monroe and the original Monroeists took pains to make it clear that it made no promise as to the international action of the United States.

. . . . .

3) *The Doctrine was perverted.* Originally it meant, "America not for Europe," but the Corollaries made it say, "America for the U.S.A." Cuba, Puerto Rico, Panama, the Dominican Republic, Haiti, Nicaragua—six United States "protectorates" in less than fifteen years. Outright interventions, with Marines landing, occupying territories, setting up governments and running the country: in Cuba from 1898 to 1903, then from 1906 to 1909, again in 1912, and finally from 1917 to 1922; in the Dominican Republic, from 1916 to 1924; in Nicaragua, from 1912 to 1933, practically without interruption; in Haiti, from 1915 to 1934. We can mention these facts because they represent a policy which belongs to the past. We *must* mention them because, since they cannot be forgotten, we expect the United States at least to admit them and never to minimize their historical significance. Wrongs belong to the past only when you are able to talk about them and still be friends. That is precisely our attitude today: do not keep wrongs bottled up inside. Friendship is a positive, driving force. Frustrated rancor cannot be taken for love. Not to fear is necessary but not sufficient. Friendship is not restraint but forward impulse.

The Monroe Doctrine is guilty—not only because it did not prevent but because it even was invoked to justify manifestations of imperialism. Rather, not the original message, but its inglorious additions. There are a good many Corollaries. I will mention the most significant ones:

In 1825, Secretary of State Clay declared that the United States could not consent to the occupation of Cuba and Puerto Rico, by "any other power than Spain." The idea was good, as is often the case in the history of Monroe's Problem Doctrine. It is better known today as the "no-transfer" principle, reiterated by Van Buren in 1829, Forsyth in 1840, Webster in 1843, and consecrated at the Havana 1940 Conference. Yet the timely warning did not apply to the United States, which, for too many years, made of Cuba a virtual protectorate. Until 1936, when Franklin D. Roosevelt's administration renounced the right of intervention granted to its country by the well-known Platt Amendment, Cuba was freed from Spain but remained subjugated to the U.S.A.

In 1845, President Polk—of whom Abraham Lincoln said,

"He feels the blood of this [Mexican] War, like the blood of Abel crying to Heaven against him"—added his Corollary, intended to justify the annexation of Texas. Said he: "We can never consent that European powers shall interfere to prevent such a union [of Texas and the United States] because it might disturb the 'balance of power,' which they [European countries] may desire to maintain upon this continent." So, having promulgated the Doctrine to redress and maintain the balance of power *in Europe,* a North American President claimed that Europe, in turn, had no right to be concerned over changes in the balance of power of the Western Hemisphere.

The second of the so-called "Grant Corollaries," in 1871 conceded the Dominican Republic the right to annex itself to the United States. President Grant stated: "I believed . . . that *our institutions were broad enough to extend over the entire continent* as rapidly as other peoples might desire to bring themselves under our protection. . . . In view of the facts which had been laid before me, and *with an earnest desire to maintain the 'Monroe Doctrine,'* I believed that I would be derelict in my duty if I did not take measures" in regard to the annexation of the Republic of Santo Domingo.

Under President Cleveland, Secretary of State Bayard said that the United States had "proclaimed herself *the protector of this Western world,* in which she is by far the strongest power." Then, in 1895, came the arrogant Olney Corollary, added by that Secretary of State who shouted to the world: "Today the United States *is practically sovereign on this continent, and its fiat is law* upon the subjects to which it confines its interposition . . . its infinite resources combined with its isolated position render it *master of the situation* and practically invulnerable as against any or all other powers. . . ." It is recorded in history as "Olney's Fiat." The word of the United States was to be a command, not only to European meddlers but to the "subjects" of Latin America's protectorates—and this bombastic attitude was based on the fact that "its infinite resources combined with its isolated position render it *master of the situation* and practically invulnerable as against any or all other powers"! How foolish it all sounds today! Nothing could be more opposed to contemporary Pan-Americanism, nothing less acceptable to Latin America. Olney's Fiat was a new expression of United States hegemony. So was the well-known Theodore Roosevelt addition: the famous Roosevelt Corollary which dealt the Doctrine its death blow.

On December 6, 1904, "Big Stick" T. R. solemnly declared:

> Any country whose people conduct themselves well, can count upon our hearty friendship. If a nation shows that it knows how to act with reasonable efficiency and decency in social and political matters, if it keeps order and pays its obligations, it need fear no interference from the United States. Chronic wrongdoing or an impotence which results in a general loosening of the ties of civilized society, may in America, as elsewhere, ultimately require intervention by some civilized nation, and in the Western Hemisphere the adherence of the United States to the Monroe Doctrine may force the United States, however reluctantly, in flagrant cases of such wrongdoing or impotence, to the exercise of an international [police] power.

No document has proved more harmful to the prestige of the United States in the Western Hemisphere. No White House policy could be more distasteful to Latin Americans—not even, perhaps, outspoken imperialism. Latin Americans are usually inclined to admire strength, force, a nation *muy hombre*. This was imperialism without military glamour: this was imperialism *à la* Tartufe, not even *à la* Napoléon. Moreover, it was a total distortion of the original message. Monroe's Doctrine was defensive and negative: defensive, in that it was essentially an opposition to eventual aggression from Europe; negative, in that it simply told Europe what it *should not* do—not what the United States *should* do. The Monroe Doctrine of later Corollaries became aggressive and positive: aggressive, because even without actual European attack, it urged United States "protection" of Latin America—and that was outright intervention; positive, because instead of telling Europe what *not* to do, it told the United States what it *should* do in the Western Hemisphere. From a case of America *vs.* Europe, the Corollaries made of the Doctrine a case of United States *vs.* America. President Monroe had merely shaken his head, brandished his finger, and said to Europe, "Now, now, gentlemen, if you meddle with us, we will not love you any more," while Teddy Roosevelt, brandishing a big stick, had shouted, "Listen, you guys, don't muscle in—this territory is ours."

. . . . .

4) Thus, in the light of historical facts—laying aside considerations of theoretical value—one can easily understand why the Monroe Doctrine became so *unpopular* not only among Latin Americans but also among an increasing number of people of the United States. Those who do not yet see the point would do well to put themselves, by a stretch of the imagination, in the victims' shoes. . . . Latin Americans, even those who admire the technical superiority of their powerful industrial neighbor, do not recognize the political or moral tutelage of the United States. We have seen that some Latin-American countries are ahead of the United States in social legislation. Mexico's agrarian policy, for instance, is certainly more advanced than that of the United States. I could name many other important fields in which Latin America maintains a moral leadership. But one should avoid unnecessary comparisons. It is enough to proclaim that Latin Americans love "life, liberty, and the pursuit of happiness" as ardently as their northern neighbors. So, any reminder directly or indirectly connected with brutal attacks from without, whoever the aggressor, automatically revives legitimate Latin-American resentment.

Many authorized spokesmen of public opinion in the United States have been as frank as Latin-American critics. On December 28, 1933, President Roosevelt, commemorating the birthday of Woodrow Wilson, admitted: "I do not hesitate to say that if I had been engaged in a political campaign as a citizen of some other American republic I might have been strongly tempted to play upon the fears of my compatriots of that republic by charging the United States of North America with some form of imperialistic desire for selfish aggrandizement."

. . . . . .

The Monroe Doctrine, with its imperialistic connotations, is loaded with the kind of explosive that endangers the Pan-American structure. That explains why United States Presidents sincerely concerned with their neighbors' feelings, from Abraham Lincoln to Franklin D. Roosevelt, have found no need to mention the Monroe Doctrine. Not even during the meeting of foreign ministers of the Americas, held at Rio de Janeiro in January 1942, did the skillful United States delegate, Sumner Welles, mention the name of that unhappy Doctrine which for the last fifty years has been the greatest stumbling block in the way of genuine inter-Americanism. And there is no doubt that the situation discussed at the Rio Conference was one which, had the message of 1823 not been perverted, would have fallen within the jurisdiction of the original Doctrine. But, right or wrong, the delegates knew that the emotional connotations of the words "Monroe Doctrine" were such that they could not be pronounced without stirring up legitimate ill feelings. *The moment Monroe's distorted shadow enters a Pan-American conference, the Good Neighbors disband.* The silence made around the Monroe Doctrine at the historical meeting at Rio is more eloquent than any indictment ever uttered against it.

5) Finally, in the light of authentic, genuine Pan-Americanism *à la* Bolívar or *à la* F. D. Roosevelt, it is obvious that the Doctrine seems completely *outmoded.* The days in which a single country—however powerful—could claim the exclusive right to behave, on the world stage, as a "rugged individualist," are gone forever. Ask Napoleon, ask the Kaiser, or ask Hitler! Civilized order is a joint enterprise, freely accepted by all partners. Mankind does not allow gangsters, be they individuals or nations. Order was established, first among the members of the family, then among the residents of the community, later among the citizens of a nation. Finally the day is near when a cooperative international order will be established among the nations of the earth. That order, whether local or national, continental or international, can be conceived only as a joint enterprise. America was the first continent in history to struggle for the establishment of such order. There can be no room in this continent for a doctrine which, even at its best and in its original intention, rests essentially on the arbitrary decision of one self-appointed "leader." The hour of selfish nationalism is past. There is no room for anarchy in organized society. Because the welfare of the many must prevail over that of the few, Monroeist Pan-Americanism has been gradually but irrevocably displaced by democratic Pan-Americanism.

The Monroe Doctrine may not be dead, but there is little use for it today. And there certainly will be less room for it in the world of tomorrow.

INTERNATIONAL
COMMUNISM
IN GUATEMALA

John Foster Dulles

One of the most serious challenges to the Monroe
Doctrine after World War II was the advent of a
Communist regime to power in Guatemala under President Jacobo Arbenz Guzmán. In countering this challenge United States Secretary of State John Foster
Dulles invoked the Monroe Doctrine, "the first and
most fundamental of our foreign policies," in the following address to the nation delivered over radio and
television on June 30, 1954. Dulles was involved in
international affairs for most of his life and became
Secretary of State in 1953, serving until his death in
1959.

Tonight I should like to talk with you about Guatemala. It
is the scene of dramatic events. They expose the evil purpose of the Kremlin to destroy the inter-American system,

John Foster Dulles, Secretary of State, address delivered to the
nation over radio and television on June 30, 1954. Washington, *Department of State Bulletin*, XXXI (July 12, 1954), 43–45.

and they test the ability of the American states to maintain the peaceful integrity of this hemisphere.

For several years international communism has been probing here and there for nesting places in the Americas. It finally chose Guatemala as a spot which it could turn into an official base from which to breed subversion which would extend to other American republics.

This intrusion of Soviet despotism was, of course, a direct challenge to our Monroe Doctrine, the first and most fundamental of our foreign policies.

It is interesting to recall that the menace which brought that Doctrine into being was itself a menace born in Russia. It was the Russian Czar Alexander and his despotic allies in Europe who, early in the last century, sought control of South America and the western part of North America. In 1823 President Monroe confronted this challenge with his declaration that the European despots could not "extend their political system to any portion of either continent without endangering our peace and happiness. We would not," he said, "behold such interposition in any form with indifference."

These sentiments were shared by the other American republics, and they were molded into a foreign policy of us all. For 131 years that policy has well served the peace and security of this hemisphere. It serves us well today.

In Guatemala, international communism had an initial success. It began ten years ago, when a revolution occurred in Guatemala. The revolution was not without justification. But the Communists seized on it, not as an opportunity for real reforms, but as a chance to gain political power.

Communist agitators devoted themselves to infiltrating the public and private organizations of Guatemala. They sent recruits to Russia and other Communist countries for revolutionary training and indoctrination in such institutions as the Lenin School at Moscow. Operating in the guise of "reformers," they organized the workers and peasants under Communist leadership. Having gained control of what they call "mass organizations," they moved on to take over the official press and radio of the Guatemalan government. They dominated the social security organization and ran the agrarian reform program. Through the technique of the "popular front" they dictated to the Congress and the President.

The judiciary made one valiant attempt to protect its integrity and independence. But the Communists, using their control of the legislative body, caused the Supreme Court to be dissolved when it refused to give approval to a Communist-contrived law. Arbenz, who until this week was President of Guatemala, was openly manipulated by the leaders of communism.

Guatemala is a small country. But its power, standing alone, is not a measure of the threat. The master plan of international communism is to gain a solid political base in this hemisphere, a base that can be used to extend Communist penetration to the other peoples of the other American governments. It was not the power of the Arbenz government that concerned us but the power behind it.

If world communism captures any American state, however small, a new and perilous front is established which will increase the danger to the entire free world and require even greater sacrifices from the American people.

This situation in Guatemala had become so dangerous that the American states could not ignore it. At Caracas last March the American states held their Tenth Inter-American Conference. They then adopted a momentous statement. They declared that "the domination or control of the political institutions of any American state by the international Communist movement . . . would constitute a threat to the sovereignty and political independence of the American states, endangering the peace of America."

There was only one American state that voted against this declaration. That state was Guatemala.

This Caracas declaration precipitated a dramatic chain of events. From their European base the Communist leaders moved rapidly to build up the military power of their agents in Guatemala. In May a large shipment of arms moved from behind the Iron Curtain into Guatemala. The shipment was sought to be secreted by false manifests and false clearances. Its ostensible destination was changed three times while en route.

At the same time, the agents of international communism in Guatemala intensified efforts to penetrate and subvert the neighboring Central American states. They attempted political assassinations and political strikes. They used consular agents for political warfare.

Many Guatemalan people protested against their being

used by Communist dictatorship to serve the Communists' lust for power. The response was mass arrests, the suppression of constitutional guaranties, the killing of opposition leaders, and other brutal tactics normally employed by communism to secure the consolidation of its power.

In the face of these events and in accordance with the spirit of the Caracas declaration, the nations of this hemisphere laid further plans to grapple with the danger. The Arbenz government responded with an effort to disrupt the inter-American system. Because it enjoyed the full support of Soviet Russia, which is on the Security Council, it tried to bring the matter before the Security Council. It did so without first referring the matter to the American regional organization as is called for both by the United Nations Charter itself and by the treaty creating the American organization.

The Foreign Minister of Guatemala openly connived in this matter with the Foreign Minister of the Soviet Union. The two were in open correspondence and ill-concealed privity. The Security Council at first voted overwhelmingly to refer the Guatemala matter to the Organization of American States. The vote was 10 to 1. But that one negative vote was a Soviet veto.

Then the Guatemalan government, with Soviet backing, redoubled its efforts to supplant the American states system by Security Council jurisdiction.

However, last Friday, the United Nations Security Council decided not to take up the Guatemalan matter but to leave it in the first instance to the American states themselves. That was a triumph for the system of balance between regional organization and world organization, which the American states had fought for when the charter was drawn up at San Francisco.

The American states then moved promptly to deal with the situation. Their peace commission left yesterday for Guatemala. Earlier the Organization of American States had voted overwhelmingly to call a meeting of their Foreign Ministers to consider the penetration of international communism in Guatemala and the measures required to eliminate it. Never before has there been so clear a call uttered with such a sense of urgency and strong resolve.

Throughout the period I have outlined, the Guatemalan government and Communist agents throughout the world have persistently attempted to obscure the real issue—that of Communist imperialism—by claiming that the United States is only interested in protecting American business. We regret that there have been disputes between the Guatemalan government and the United Fruit Company. We have urged repeatedly that these disputes be submitted for settlement to an international tribunal or to international arbitration. That is the way to dispose of problems of this sort. But this issue is relatively unimportant. All who know the temper of the United States people and government must realize that our overriding concern is that which, with others, we recorded at Caracas, namely, the endangering by international communism of the peace and security of this hemisphere.

The people of Guatemala have now been heard from. Despite the armaments piled up by the Arbenz government, it was unable to enlist the spiritual cooperation of the people.

Led by Colonel Castillo Armas, patriots arose in Guatemala to challenge the Communist leadership—and to change it. Thus, the situation is being cured by the Guatemalans themselves.

Last Sunday, President Arbenz of Guatemala resigned and seeks asylum. Others are following his example.

Tonight, just as I speak, Colonel Castillo Armas is in conference in El Salvador with Colonel Monzón, the head of the Council which has taken over the power in Guatemala City. It was this power that the just wrath of the Guatemalan people wrested from President Arbenz, who then took flight.

Now the future of Guatemala lies at the disposal of the Guatemalan people themselves. It lies also at the disposal of leaders loyal to Guatemala who have not treasonably become the agents of an alien despotism which sought to use Guatemala for its own evil ends.

The events of recent months and days add a new and glorious chapter to the already great tradition of the American states.

Each one of the American states has cause for profound gratitude. We can all be grateful that we showed at Caracas an impressive solidarity in support of our American institutions. I may add that we are prepared to do so again at the

conference called for Rio. Advance knowledge of that solidarity undoubtedly shook the Guatemalan government.

We can be grateful that the Organization of American
States showed that it could act quickly and vigorously in aid
of peace. There was proof that our American organization is
not just a paper organization, but that it has vigor and
vitality to act.

We can be grateful to the United Nations Security Council, which recognized the right of regional organizations in
the first instance to order their own affairs. Otherwise the
Soviet Russians would have started a controversy which
would have set regionalism against universality and gravely
wounded both.

Above all, we can be grateful that there were loyal citizens of Guatemala who, in the face of terrorism and violence and against what seemed insuperable odds, had the
courage and the will to eliminate the traitorous tools of
foreign despots.

The need for vigilance is not past. Communism is still a
menace everywhere. But the people of the United States
and of the other American republics can feel tonight that at
least one grave danger has been averted. Also an example is
set which promises increased security for the future. The
ambitious and unscrupulous will be less prone to feel that
communism is the wave of their future.

In conclusion, let me assure the people of Guatemala. As
peace and freedom are restored to that sister republic, the
government of the United States will continue to support
the just aspirations of the Guatemalan people. A prosperous
and progressive Guatemala is vital to a healthy hemisphere.
The United States pledges itself not merely to political opposition to communism but to help to alleviate conditions in
Guatemala and elsewhere which might afford communism
an opportunity to spread its tentacles throughout the hemisphere. Thus we shall seek in positive ways to make our
Americas an example which will inspire men everywhere.

AN INTERNATIONAL
AGREEMENT

Danton Jobim

Danton Jobim (1906–   ), a Brazilian journalist and
lawyer, in the following selection from his book *O Ciclo
da Doutrina de Monroe* traces the transformation of the
Monroe Doctrine into an international doctrine of the
Americas. In 1932 Jobim became editor-in-chief of
Diário Carioca, one of the most influential newspapers
of Rio de Janeiro.

In December 1933 Franklin Delano Roosevelt, as President,
solemnly declared that

> the definite policy of the United States from now on is
> one opposed to armed intervention. The maintenance
> of constitutional government in other nations is not a
> sacred obligation devolving upon the United States
> alone. The maintenance of law and of the orderly proc-
> esses of government in this hemisphere is the concern
> of each individual nation within its own borders first of
> all. It is only if and when the failure of orderly proc-

Danton Jobim, *O Ciclo da Doutrina de Monroe* (Rio de Janeiro:
Ediçoes Souza, 1955), pp. [95]–106. Translated by the editor.

esses affects the other nations of the continent that it becomes their concern; and the point to stress is that in such an event it becomes the joint concern of a whole continent, in which we are all neighbors.

In that historic discourse the President of the United States consecrated the principle of "joint responsibility," repudiating the unilateral action which characterized the Monroe Doctrine for more than a century.

In 1934 the American Senate approved the resolution of the Inter-American Conference at Montevideo (1933) against the intervention of any state in the internal or external affairs of another. In the conference which met in 1936 in Buenos Aires on the initiative of the American government, that principle was reaffirmed with greater force, creating a basis for the later Declaration of Lima of 1938, which assumed greater dramatic importance as we then found ourselves only a few steps from a new world conflagration arising from the words and deeds of the Nazi government. . . .

     . . . . .

Finally, in 1938 at the eighth Inter-American Conference, convened in Peru, the celebrated Declaration of Lima crowned the movement for the continentalization of the Monroe Doctrine. Confronted with the activities of the totalitarian states in the Americas, the United States brought about the adoption at Lima of an energetic declaration of opposition to those activities. In doing so the United States responded to the desires of the [Latin-American] states, showing that now it was more interested in reversing the terms of its traditional policy and achieving the complete victory of the principle of joint responsibility in the defense of the continent. All the republics must take their positions in protecting the independence of the Americas, enlisting themselves in a true alliance. No longer guardianship or wards, but participation of one and all in the security system.

The declaration of solidarity in the face of external dangers is implemented with the conventions of collective security, of neutrality, and with the protocol of nonintervention.

As for the Declaration of Lima, of November [December] 24, 1938, reaffirming the absolute sovereignty of the twenty-one nations, it expresses their determination to defend themselves against foreign interventions and to present a united front against them. The American nations reaffirm, on the other hand, their firm intention to consult mutually among themselves in cases in which the peace, the security, or the territorial integrity of any of them is threatened.

Thus the understanding and the application of the Monroe Doctrine passed, in a little more than a century, through three distinct phases, which we can summarize as follows: 1. the negative phase: the veto opposing any European intervention in the affairs or the destiny of the peoples of America, which was the real sense of the message of 1823; 2. the imperialist phase: initiated as the policy of force by Theodore Roosevelt which was especially directed toward the Central American countries and which gained its impulse with the construction of the Panama Canal; 3. finally, the phase of the return to the Doctrine in its original defensive meaning, which commenced in the Hoover presidency, with the publication of the Clark Memorandum.

With the return to its original meaning the Monroe Doctrine practically disappears, losing its reason for existence as a political principle and retaining only a purely historical significance. The United States has become the major world power and today exercises the leadership of the nations which have escaped Soviet influence, the so-called free world. They are involved in so many alliances both inside and outside our continent that it would be difficult to enumerate them.

The Monroe Doctrine was founded upon geographical realities—the isolation of the Americas by the oceans—and upon political realities—European colonialism. Both have disappeared. Now it is not only the security of the Americas that the United States is charged with guarding but the security of the whole free world. It is not now only the Latin-American republics which need the military and economic protection of the United States but all the nations which are located outside the circuit of the Iron Curtain.

During the last war the Nazis were prepared to come to Dakar, where they could easily attack the eastern part of Brazil in which the Americans had one terminus of their "Corridor of Victory." . . .

The war, however, not only destroyed the primacy of Europe in the world, but shook its colonial systems to their foundations. The thing that rises today as a menace to the peace and security of America, in this era of total war, is the

Soviet Union with its new type of imperialism, namely ideological, of which international fascism was only a pallid
imitation. The struggle against that aggressive power demands a flexible front which is at the same time both very
near and very distant, inside our house and in the farthest
reaches of the world, as the cases of Korea and Guatemala
demonstrated. Franklin Roosevelt said, at the beginning of
the last war, that the frontiers of America were on the
Rhine. Today they are everywhere, wherever Communist
expansion is attempting to extend its dominion, in France,
in Austria, in Iran, and in Malaysia, as well as in Korea. The
Monroe Doctrine can no longer protect the hemisphere, for
isolation is impossible, and the hemisphere is involved in
international pacts of all kinds, demonstrating the indivisi-
bility of the free world.

The last open reference to the Monroe Doctrine officially
made in connection with an international question by the
American government was the exasperated declaration directed at the Russians by the then Under Secretary of State
[sic] Henry Cabot Lodge in a meeting of the Security
Council of the United Nations in the case of Guatemala in
1954: "Stay out of the Western Hemisphere. Stay out of this
hemisphere. Don't try to start your plans and conspiracies
here."

The complexity of the international situation and American leadership of the non-Communist world argues against
that allusion to the Monroe principle. Daniel James in his
book *Red Design for the Americas: Guatemalan Prelude*
declared correctly:

Lodge was merely reaffirming the Monroe Doctrine.
But the occasion and manner in which he did so were
ill-advised; for the sole result was to lend justification
to the Red cry, Asia for the Asians, at a time when the
United States was deeply involved in the Indo-China
war as well as other Asian situations.

On the other hand, it is evident that the Guatemalan case
was scarcely only a local episode but rather a skirmish in the
vast and formless front of Communist aggression, an incident capable of putting into action not only the machinery
of Pan-American security but even that of the United Nations itself. Elsewhere the position of the Organization of

American States toward that front was clearly defined when the Conference at Bogotá in 1948 [Caracas in 1954] approved the Declaration of Solidarity for the Preservation of the Political Integrity of the American States against the Intervention of International Communism. An intervention of that nature is the only one which in the present epoch can be considered possible, at least so long as there do not arise other nations on this planet which dispute with the United States and with the Soviet Union the indisputable leadership which they enjoy in their respective spheres of influence.

By becoming internationalized, the Monroe Doctrine thus lost its great characteristic features: the abstention from involvement in questions outside the Americas, the resistance to European aggressions, and unilateralness in its application. The United States does not now need to invoke it in its relations with other peoples, for it is embodied in precise diplomatic instruments; it has ceased to be a simple political declaration and has become an international agreement. It was the past experience in implementing that Doctrine that inspired the policy of regional agreements of mutual defense outside the American continent through the active participation of the United States. Thus, many European nations signed with the American government in 1949 the North Atlantic Pact in which, repeating what the American republics had done at Lima eleven years before, they agreed that an attack on one of the signatories would be considered an attack on all the others.

The era of the Jeffersonian principle—"no entangling alliances"—has passed. But the doctrine of Monroe and Adams which was at the same time both practical and idealistic has not disappeared at all. It survives in its true sense concealed under other names and other forms, bearing fruit in other parts of the world as the highest and finest contribution of the Americas to international law.

Political principles are not eternal; they last as long as the conditions which created them continue. But when they are useful and just they die gloriously so that they become transfigured and converted into new principles broadening their radius of influence to such an extent and by such means that they cease longer to be recognizable.

AN UNDEFINED
DOCTRINE

Isidro Fabela

Despite the endorsement of the principles of the Monroe Doctrine by all the American states after World War II, the Mexican author Isidro Fabela (1882–1964), acknowledging that it remained a unilateral doctrine of the United States, insisted upon its further clarification either by the United States Congress or, preferably, by a special Pan-American congress. Dr. Fabela was closely associated with the Carranza regime and represented Mexico in many diplomatic posts between 1915 and 1921. His published works include *Los Estados Unidos Contra la Libertad* (1920) and *Las Doctrinas Monroe y Drago* (1957), from which the following selection is taken.

Mr. Monroe in his message of 1823 laid down four principles relating to the international policy of his country.

First: The United States had not intervened and will not intervene in the European colonies already established in America.

Isidro Fabela, *Las Doctrinas Monroe y Drago* (Mexico: Universidad Nacional Autónoma de Mexico, 1957), pp. 7–13. Translated by the editor, and reprinted by permission of the publisher.

Second: The United States will not intervene in the internal affairs of the European powers.

Third: The United States will not permit new European colonization in America.

Fourth: The United States will oppose European interventions in the Latin-American republics.

These four points constitute the essence of the prolix Presidential message of 1823, which contains the badly named Monroe Doctrine, because it is neither a doctrine of international law nor is it exclusively Monroe's. It is necessary therefore to declare emphatically that all the enumerated international postulates which North American statesmen have affirmed and are affirming with so much enthusiasm and strong popular support, all of them, without exception, have often gone unfulfilled through oversight and on other occasions have been violated by either European or United States actions, as we are going to show.

But, first of all, let us analyze it: Which of these questions of policy or of international law constitutes the Doctrine? Do the four points? Or one of them only? Or ought the whole message to be called the Monroe Doctrine?

We do not know, despite the fact that President Wilson gave the Doctrine an official interpretation.

In fact, when at the request of that President the Doctrine was included in the Covenant of the League of Nations, the government of the Republic of El Salvador sent a note to him in Washington asking him to be good enough "to define the authentic concept of the Doctrine not only as it is understood in the present but also in its future projections."

To this pertinent question of the Salvadoran chancellery, Secretary of State Robert Lansing answered:

The opinion of this government was expressed by the President (Mr. Wilson) in his address at the Second Pan-American Scientific Congress, in which are found the following paragraphs:

The Monroe Doctrine was proclaimed by the United States on her own authority. It always has been maintained and always will be maintained upon her own responsibility. But the Monroe Doctrine demanded merely that European governments should not attempt to extend their political systems to this side of the Atlantic. It did not disclose the use which the United

States intended to make of her power on this side of the Atlantic. It was a hand held up in warning, but there was no promise in it of what America was going to do with the implied and partial protectorate which she apparently was trying to set up on this side of the water; and I believe you will sustain me in the statement that it has been fears and suspicions which have hitherto prevented the greater intimacy and confidence and trust between the Americas.

That declaration, notwithstanding that it was made by the Executive, cannot be taken as the official interpretation of the famous Doctrine, because it expresses the opinion of the President who uttered it; not that of all the Presidents, nor even that of all the governments of the United States.

According to the governmental system of that country, the declaration of Mr. Wilson does not obligate either him personally, nor the United States government, nor even the future Presidents of that republic.

In order that the entire world, and particularly the Latin-American peoples, may reliably obtain a clear and precise idea of the Doctrine and its scope, it would be necessary that the Congress of the American Union define it, giving to diplomatic history and the law of nations its concrete and authentic interpretation, single and definitive, as Pan-American policy and international justice require.

But the Congress of the United States has never given that interpretation, nor is it likely to do so while the spirit of imperialism prevails in that nation; because the political force of the Doctrine lies precisely in its lack of definition and in its elasticity, with the result that sometimes it is interpreted in one sense and sometimes in a very different sense as suits a strong-minded President or the political party in power, or as seems required by the expansionist and hegemonic designs of the White House.

If the Monroe Doctrine were defined by means of a decree or a joint declaration of Congress which would incorporate the international laws of the United States, all the Latin-American fears and suspicions would diminish insofar as they result from the interpretation of the Doctrine, and there would remain only as an important question for Latin America the matter of strict compliance with the definition given. It is clearly understood, of course, that that definition should not deviate in its elements from the original thought of the authors [of the Doctrine], which never was, as we have seen, contrary to the international law of the Hispanic-American states, since it only reaffirmed its respect for the old and recognized juridical principle of *nonintervention*.

It follows then that the only way in which the entire continent can be reconciled to the existence and application of the Monroe Doctrine would be to study it, to discuss it, and to interpret it in a special Pan-American congress, which would include all the nations of the New World, since it is logical and fair to insist that if it concerns all the American states the governments of those states without exception ought to express their views on the matter and give their approval as to what the Monroe Doctrine should be in the future as well as the way in which it is to be understood and applied for the benefit of all the peoples of America.

But since, unhappily, the various administrations in the United States have always shown an unwillingness to discuss that question, considering it to be only national and not essentially continental, it results that in fact the Monroe Doctrine is invoked, interpreted, and applied by the United States whenever it suits its convenience, without any consultation with the Ibero-American chancelleries, as if the political jurisdiction of Washington included all this part of the globe, from Canada to the Argentine republic, and as if a government had the right to establish international political systems without the consent of the nations most concerned.

The United States interprets the so-called Monroe Doctrine every time an international incident occurs in America, and it is unnecessary to say that each interpretation is adjusted to the requirements of the moment, as a result of which almost all the interpretations differ from each other. In every case, throughout the long history of the Doctrine, one observes clearly this one tendency and single objective: to favor the interests of the United States to the exclusion of the interests of those of any other country, whether American or not, even when it apparently is pursuing a disinterested end.

THE MONROE DOCTRINE
AND PAN-AMERICANISM

Simón Planas-Suárez

In a book entitled *Les Principes Américains de Politique Internationale et la Doctrine de Monroe,* published in 1959, Dr. Planas-Suárez, whose earlier favorable interpretation of the Monroe Doctrine is presented
in a selection on pages 105–109, analyzes the relation
of the Monroe Doctrine to Pan-Americanism. His conclusions are as follows:

---

1. The declaration of international policy [which was]
made by the President of the United States in his message
of 1823 and which has received the name Monroe Doctrine
has its source in the principles proclaimed and defended by
the Americans of the South as well as those of the North,
even before being announced by Monroe.

2. The Latin-American nations have the right and the
moral duty to declare, either individually or collectively, the
interpretation, the import, and the application which they
will give to American principles of international policy when

Simón Planas-Suárez, *Les Principes Américains de Politique Internationale et la Doctrine de Monroe* (Geneva: Imprimerie de "La
Tribune de Genève," 1959), pp. 117–119. Translated by the editor.

they are concerned with inter-American relations or with matters in which they are involved with the powers of other continents, just as the United States did in the message of President Monroe and on other more recent occasions.

3. The Monroe Doctrine, having been proclaimed by a strong nation, was able, by respecting the principles of independent sovereignty and territorial integrity of the American states, to render a direct and immediate service to those states, enabling them to consolidate their independence and to affirm their international personality.

4. The Monroe Doctrine, though it was an individual and restricted declaration, established a formula of independence which is considered as a postulate of international character accepted by all civilized nations: it is in this sense that one can speak of its extension to South [Latin] America.

5. The principles of international law which assure to states juridical and political equality, independent sovereignty, non-intervention, and the mutual guaranty of territorial integrity, principles proclaimed by all the *Latin-American* republics, find broad and efficacious expression in the Doctrine of Bolívar which, by its nature, extends to the entire world and is known as the Monroe Doctrine.

6. The name Monroe Doctrine is individual because this is the name which the United States gives to the individual declaration of international policy made in the Presidential message of 1823; the other republics of the continent neither can nor should adopt it to designate the principles of international American policy which they proclaim and defend; from which it follows that the Monroe Doctrine is in no sense a regional understanding among the American republics, as it was erroneously called in the Covenant of the League of Nations.

7. The Monroe Doctrine and the positive international policy of the United States are two things completely different: the latter evolves according to circumstances and occasions; it is therefore variable, whereas the former is immutable.

It is, then, an error to confuse two notions which are so distinct and to call Monroe Doctrine every action or every attitude of the United States in relation to the other American republics, since nothing more is involved than the determination of their *positive international policy,* a policy which, naturally, the other nations of the continent can approve or disapprove. They are free either to accommodate themselves to it or to protest against it; in any case that policy is foreign to the Monroe Doctrine and is carried out completely independent of it.

THE UNITED STATES
REAFFIRMS THE
MONROE DOCTRINE

State Department

The United States became seriously concerned when Fidel Castro, after seizing power in Cuba in January 1959, proceeded to swing his country, situated almost within sight of southern Florida, into the orbit of Soviet Communism. The United States was publicly warned in mid-1960 by the head of Soviet Russia, Nikita Khrushchev, that "if the United States imperialists take aggressive action against the Cuban people, who are defending their national independence, we will support the Cuban people." This offer of aid was coupled with Soviet denunciation of the Monroe Doctrine as "dead." To this charge the State Department replied in the following press release, dated July 14, 1960, explicitly reaffirming the Monroe Doctrine as a policy of the United States.

Department of State, "U.S. Reaffirms Principles of Monroe Doctrine," Press Release 392, dated July 14, 1960, *Department of State Bulletin*, XLIII (August 1, 1960), 170–171.

In his remarks concerning the Monroe Doctrine at his press conference on July 12, Mr. Khrushchev again displayed his extraordinary ability to ignore facts.

In the first place, the principles of the Monroe Doctrine are as valid to-day as they were in 1823 when the Doctrine was proclaimed. Furthermore, the Monroe Doctrine's purpose of preventing any extension to this hemisphere of a despotic political system contrary to the independent status of the American states is supported by the inter-American security system through the Organization of American States. Specifically the Organization of American States Charter and the Rio Treaty provide the means for common action to protect the hemisphere against the interventionist and aggressive designs of international communism. Likewise, Mr. Khrushchev failed to mention that the Rio Treaty is the first of the regional treaties for which provision is made under article 51 of the United Nations Charter.

Mr. Khrushchev might appropriately reflect on the fact that one of the considerations for establishing the Rio Treaty was that:

> . . . the American regional community affirms as a manifest truth that juridical organization is a necessary prerequisite of security and peace, and that peace is founded on justice and moral order and, consequently, on the international recognition and protection of human rights and freedoms, on the indispensable well-being of the people, and on the effectiveness of democracy for the international realization of justice and security. . . .

One of the principal purposes of the Rio Treaty was to provide a method for dealing with threats of imperialistic powers seeking to establish their domination in the Western Hemisphere.

A further remarkable development was revealed in Mr. Khrushchev's meeting with the press. Speaking as the Head of the Soviet government, he arrogated to himself the power to determine what international agreements should or should not be binding—even though the Soviet Union is not a party thereto. In this particular instance it was not only the Rio Treaty but also the treaty between the United States and Cuba covering Guantánamo which he has sought to abrogate. While disregard for treaties to which it is a party may be viewed by the U.S.S.R. as a convenient approach to international relations, such an effort can only be regarded by law-abiding states as another example of Soviet intervention in the affairs of other countries.

Mr. Khrushchev's latest references to U.S.-Cuban relations are of a piece with his threat of July 9. As a pretext for his threat, he conjured up the straw man of a non-existent menace of U.S. aggression against Cuba.

The threat of the use of force, made so blatantly by the Soviet Chairman in relation to the affairs of nations of the Western Hemisphere, is contrary to the basic principle of the United Nations Charter which rejects the use of force in the settlement of international disputes. This naked menace to world peace, brandished so callously by the Soviet leader, reveals the hypocrisy of his protestations in behalf of peace.

Moreover, these statements of Mr. Khrushchev appear to be designed to establish a "Bolshevik doctrine" providing for the use of Soviet military power in support of Communist movements anywhere in the world. Mr. Khrushchev speaks approvingly of the historically positive role of the Monroe Doctrine during the 19th century, when it was applied against the European imperialisms of that day, but declares that "everything has changed abruptly" now that it stands in the way of the new imperialism: international communism.

The principles which the United States government enunciated in the face of the attempts of the old imperialism to intervene in the affairs of this hemisphere are as valid today for the attempts of the new imperialism. It consequently reaffirms with vigor the principles expressed by President Monroe:

> We owe it . . . to candor . . . to declare that we should consider any attempt on their [European powers] part to extend their system to any portion of this hemisphere as dangerous to our peace and safety.

Today, nearly a century and a half later, the United States is gratified that these principles are not professed by itself alone but represent through solemn agreements the views of the American community as a whole.

SENATE DEBATE ON THE CUBAN CRISIS, 1962

The missile build-up in Cuba by the Soviets in 1962 revived discussion of the Monroe Doctrine. It inspired the following debate in the Senate on September 10, participated in by Senator Thomas Dodd (D-Conn), Senator Kenneth Keating (R-NY), and Senator Wayne Morse (D-Ore).

Mr. DODD. Mr. President, over the past several weeks some of our most distinguished Senators have made statements on the subject of Cuba, expressing diverse opinions. This is as it should be, if the Senate is truly to fulfill its advisory function in the critical realm of foreign affairs. . . .

Three and a half years ago, Fidel Castro and a band of several thousand guerrilla followers were made masters of Cuba when the dictatorial regime of Fulgencio Batista crumbled. . . .

Today Castro's Cuba is as completely communized as the Soviet Union or Red China. The Iron Curtain has been rung down 90 miles from our shores. . . .

The Batista regime crumbled primarily because it was venal and inept and cruel, and had lost popular support. But it was American policy that was responsible for the timing of Batista's downfall and for the fact that, when he fell, the only man who could fill the vacuum that was created was Fidel Castro. . . .

Like all my colleagues, I have given much thought to the situation in Cuba. I should like to submit for their consideration a six-point plan of action for the liberation of Cuba. . . .

I believe the first measure we must take is to commit ourselves to a "declaration of independence and freedom for the Cuban people," so that the whole world will know that the decision has been made to completely eradicate the malignancy of Castroism.

Second, I believe that we should inform the Cuban exiles in this country that we are prepared to support the establishment of, and grant recognition to, a broadly representative provisional Cuban government-in-exile. If the Cuban political leaders cannot achieve the minimum agreement essential to the establishment of such a provisional government, then I believe that the faculty of the University of Havana, most of which is now in this country, or alternatively, the several hundred members of the Havana Bar Association who have sought refuge here, should be constituted as a provisional government, committed to the holding of free elections within one year of the liberation of Cuba.

As a third and immediate measure—in anticipation of action by the Organization of American States—I believe we should invoke the Monroe Doctrine to proclaim a total embargo on shipments of Communist military materials and military personnel to Cuba.

The words of President Monroe never had clearer application than they have today in Cuba.

In his message to Congress on December 2, 1823, President Monroe asserted—

> as a principle in which the rights and interests of the United States are involved, that the American continents, by the free and independent condition which they have assumed and maintain, are henceforth not to be considered as subjects for future colonization by any European power [*sic,* powers].

We owe it therefore to candor, and to the amicable

relations existing between the United States and those [European] powers, to declare that we should consider any attempt on their part to extend their system to any portion of this hemisphere, as dangerous to our peace and safety—

I ask my colleagues to note carefully the wording of this statement, to note that President Monroe spoke of extending—

their system to any portion of this hemisphere.

I would also ask them to note with care the words of President Monroe when he said further in his statement that the United States would view as an unfriendly act

any interposition for the purpose of oppressing them— the Latin-American republics—or controlling in any other manner, their destiny by any European power.

I believe that this wording applies clearly to the situation that exists in Cuba today. I cannot understand, indeed, how my good friend, the distinguished Senator from California [Mr. Engle], could take the stand that the Monroe Doctrine did not apply to Cuba because the Soviet armaments and Soviet personnel now in that country were there by virtue of an official request from the government of Cuba. He stated:

The Monroe Doctrine applies to a situation in which a foreign power by force overthrows an established regime in this hemisphere.

As I read the Monroe Doctrine, it applies to "any interposition" for the purpose of oppressing the Latin-American peoples or controlling their destiny "in any other manner."

Nor can I understand the legitimacy which he accords the Castro government in his statement. The Castro government was not elected by the people of Cuba and does not represent them. It is not an indigenous government, but a quisling Soviet regime which has been imposed on the Cuban people by deception and by fraud and by terror, and which now maintains itself in power only thanks to the massive presence of Soviet arms.

At the time President Monroe made his historic declaration, the United States was only a minor power compared with the great nations of Europe, and its navy was by no means the first in the world. Today we are indisputably the world's greatest power, while our navy dwarfs the navies of all the Communist nations combined. If the Monroe Doctrine cannot be enforced today to deal with a situation that more clearly violates its intent than has any other situation since its proclamation, then I say that the candid thing to do would be to strike the Doctrine from our books.

It is, however, my confident expectation that, with or without the support of our Latin-American neighbors, the wisdom of the Monroe Doctrine in its specific application to Cuba will be recognized, and the necessary action will be taken to implement it.

In invoking the Monroe Doctrine to prevent the shipment of Communist military materials and military personnel to Cuba we could, I am certain, make it abundantly clear that our action was directed not against the Cuban people but against the Soviet quisling regime. We might even give consideration to substituting a food ship, loaded with American surplus food, for every shipment of Communist arms of military contraband that was turned back.

Fourth, I believe that we should greatly intensify our entire propaganda effort with the frankly declared purpose of assisting the Cuban people to liberate themselves. We must direct this propaganda not merely to the people of Cuba, but to all the peoples of the Americas, documenting the facts about Castro's communism, about the treachery by which he imposed his Communist tyranny on the Cuban people, about the abandoned promises for free elections, about the catastrophic economic mismanagement that characterizes his regime, about the thousands of Soviet and Chinese experts who are now flooding the country, about the abject economic and political tutelage to the Soviet Union into which Castro has led Cuba.

As a fifth step, I believe we should be prepared, preferably in concert with the OAS nations, to impose a total blockade on all shipments to Cuba, other than shipments of food and consumer goods.

Sixth, I believe we should be prepared to give open and increasing assistance to Cuba's heroic freedom fighters, who are daily defying Castro's execution squads.

I note that there have been some editorials in our country

which have deplored the action of the group of Cuban refugee students who recently bombarded Havana from makeshift craft that they had sailed from Miami.

According to these editorials, the United States government should now take the most stringent action to prevent any such future expeditions by Cuban patriots operating from our shores. I would point out to these editors that none of them, to my knowledge, made similar protests when the Castro movement was seeking to overthrow the Batista regime, and when agents for the Castro movement were active in this country, raising funds for its support and purchasing arms and ammunition which they sent by plane and by ship to the Castro guerrillas from Florida ports. Indeed, it is amazing, in retrospect, to realize that there was no public protest over the virtually total suspension of American law enforcement when it was a matter of "arms for Castro."

I suggest that it is our moral duty to give the Cuban freedom fighters of today at least the same leeway that we gave the agents of Castro only several years ago. Indeed, I would urge that we not only support the resistance movement in Cuba, but that we openly support the creation of a "Cuban Freedom Legion" in exile, whose ranks would be open to all Latin-American nationals.

To be realistic, we cannot completely exclude the possibility of military assistance to the Cuban freedom fighters. But I believe that this is a decision that can only be made at a later date and against the background of a plan of action similar to the one I have here outlined.

Let us not be deterred from a policy of liberation by the fact that the Communist nations and certain of the Afro-Asian nations will scream at the top of their lungs that American imperialism is engaging in military aggression.

It is the Soviet Union which stands convicted of political and military aggression in Cuba, and which, from its Cuban beachhead, is daily practicing political aggression against the countries of the Western Hemisphere.

Moreover, the Soviets and the Afro-Asian extremists have long ago forfeited all right to protest against unilateral military action.

A free Hungary threatened no one; but, in open defiance of the United Nations, the Soviet Union sent in an army of

5,000 tanks to crush the Hungarian revolution in blood and to impose an inglorious quisling regime which could not have mustered 100 votes in the whole of Hungary.

Goa threatened no one; but, in violation of the United Nations Charter, India invaded and annexed the territory of Goa.

West New Guinea, as a colony of the Netherlands, threatened no one, and the Netherlands government had already committed itself to a policy of self-determination for the Papuan people. But Indonesia has now succeeded in forcing the peaceful surrender of west New Guinea to Sukarno's imperialist ambitions, flagrantly violating the two cardinal tenets on which the United Nations is founded—the right of self-determination of peoples and the repudiation of force as an instrument for the settlement of disputes.

Let us not be deterred from our commitment to a free and independent Cuba by the hysterical protests of tyrants or opportunists who usurp the name of the Cuban people or hypocritically invoke the United Nations Charter. For I believe that the justice of this policy of liberation will be vindicated by the Cuban people themselves in free elections, under OAS auspices, on the morrow after their liberation.

. . . . .

Mr. KEATING. I am sorry that every member of the Senate was not present to hear the analysis of the situation in Cuba delivered by the distinguished Senator from Connecticut.

The Senator from Connecticut has advanced a program which does not involve armed action against Cuba at this time, action which I think most of us would agree would be a mistake; but he does set forth a six-point program, clearly after considerable study. There are two points about the Senator's address to which I should like to add a word.

One has to do with the analysis which the Senator from Connecticut has made of the nature of the weapons which are now located in the advanced Soviet base which is Cuba, weapons which cannot in any sense be considered purely defensive. Whether a weapon is defensive or offensive depends entirely upon the triggerman or the operator of the particular weapon and the person or the nation against which the weapon is turned. True, Mig fighters, tanks, missiles, antiaircraft guns, and torpedo boats are defensive weapons; but they are also offensive if the desire is to use them offensively.

The other point relates to the analysis of the Monroe Doctrine. As the Senator has said, it was contended by the distinguished Senator from California [Mr. Engle] and has also been contended by others—and I venture to say that the Senator from California was enunciating the present policy of this administration—that the Monroe Doctrine is not here involved because Soviet Russia was invited to Cuba by the existing government of Cuba.

Think what that reasoning leads to. It means that in any Latin-American country, all that needs to happen is a *coup d'état*, following which the government which takes over by force may call in Soviet Russia or Communist China, or some other Communist country; and thereby the Monroe Doctrine will not apply. At present the situation is the Monroe Doctrine minus one country; and the next country which has a *coup d'état* will make the situation the Monroe Doctrine minus two. Pretty soon, all that will be left will be the Monroe Doctrine applying to the United States of America.

President Monroe made it abundantly clear that if the Monroe Doctrine is to remain in force—and I do not believe it is the policy of the United States to have it junked—it should cover cases in which our southern brethren—meaning the Latin-American republics—had imposed upon them by force from the outside the ideologies and the principles of a foreign power, which they would not of their own accord adopt. That is exactly what has happened in Cuba. Today Cuba is a Communist state; and communism was imposed upon Cuba by the world Communist movement, of which it is now apparent that Fidel Castro is a part, and admittedly so. Castro and Khrushchev have had the effrontery not only to admit but also to boast that they are making a military base of Cuba and are increasing military supplies and military personnel there.

. . . . . .

Mr. MORSE. One of the most delicate problems we have—it is very risky even to comment on it publicly, but it should be commented on—is the problem involving the Monroe Doctrine. The Monroe Doctrine is not dead, but I do not think the Monroe Doctrine is the doctrine it was when it was first established by the United States, or when we enforced it fifty or seventy-five years ago. In part—and note my language—it was established in order to guarantee to our neighbors to the south of us that we would protect them, as well as ourselves, from any possible overrunning of them, or any one of them, by a foreign power.

We carried that out, although, as we know, the historians have written that in the early decades we carried it out through the British fleet. After all, our great ally, Great Britain, enforced the Monroe Doctrine for a good many years, in that other foreign nations knew if they sought to exercise any extraterritorial ambitions over Latin America we would stand firm on the Monroe Doctrine but the Monroe Doctrine would, in those days, be enforced by the British fleet.

A great many changes have occurred since the initiation of the Monroe Doctrine. For example, the section which declares that we will not become involved in European affairs is a completely dead letter. Insofar as it relates to this hemisphere, it is a two-pronged Doctrine; and let us never forget it. It is a Doctrine in which we made clear that from the standpoint of our own national security we did not propose to have foreign powers establish extraterritorial rights in the Western Hemisphere. But we also said we were opposed to that because we were going to protect our neighbors to the south who, in that time of history, were exceedingly weak nations and could have been easily overrun if they could not rely upon their great neighbor to the north to come to their defense and assistance if necessary.

In our conferences in Latin America for some time past we have found that the attitude of our Latin-American friends today in some instances is not the attitude they adopted at the time the Monroe Doctrine was first initiated. This is a delicate subject, but some of them have taken the position—and it is well recognized—that any carrying out of any policy of the Monroe Doctrine as originally contemplated by the United States, so far as Latin-American countries are concerned, would have to be done with their complete consent, cooperation, and association. In other words, the Latin Americans question the right of the United States to take the position that it can say to any foreign power, "Your relationships with country X, Y, or Z in Latin

America are going to be determined by the United States."

So we enter into areas of conflict, which require the exercise of very delicate diplomacy.

During World War II, we negotiated a series of treaties and declarations by Western Hemisphere nations which sought to make incursions by Axis powers into the hemisphere the subject of combined opposition and resistance by the signatories.

We sought, in other words, to enforce the Monroe Doctrine not unilaterally, but through hemispheric action.

That is how we changed the concept of the Monroe Doctrine during World War II relative to the German-Italian-Japanese axis.

Since then, we have done much the same thing relative to communism. We have held a series of conferences in an effort to keep communism out of this hemisphere not simply as United States policy and by United States action but as a policy and action of the Organization of American States.

I do not know of any country which signed the act of Punta del Este which would not want to cooperate with us in stemming the establishment of communism in Latin America by way either of a beachhead in Cuba or of a Communist taking over of X, Y, or Z country in Latin America, for there is a recognition that if that should happen in Latin America to one country, or to two or three, it could very well extend through the hemisphere.

There have been in the press some rather excited editorials whose writers have not taken into account that the Monroe Doctrine today is not the Monroe Doctrine established by President Monroe, because of these changes in the attitude of some of our Latin-American friends in regard to the applicability of the Monroe Doctrine to certain types of facts now. I only mention it in passing in this discussion, because it ought to be noted in the *Record*.

THE MONROE DOCTRINE:
A SOVIET VIEW

Basil Dmytryshyn and
Jesse L. Gilmore

"The Monroe Doctrine is dead," pronounced Nikita
Khrushchev. Therefore, he added, it "should best be
buried . . . so it does not poison the air by its decay."

Professors Basil Dmytryshyn and Jesse L. Gilmore of
Portland State College in Oregon analyze, in the fol-
lowing study, changing Soviet attitudes toward the
Doctrine.

The Soviet view of the Monroe Doctrine has passed through
two distinct phases of development: from 1918 to 1945 and
from 1945 to the present. Before World War II, Soviet
interest in the Monroe Doctrine, as revealed through their
publications, was extremely limited. While it is difficult to
determine the exact reason for this absence of interest, it is
highly probable that the lack of qualified scholars, the pre-

Basil Dmytryshyn and Jesse L. Gilmore, "The Monroe Doctrine: a
Soviet View," *Bulletin: Institute for the Study of the USSR*, Munich,
Germany, XI (May 1964), 3-14. Reprinted by permission of the pub-
lisher.

occupation with domestic policies, the struggle for security, and the efforts to gain the support of and recognition by the United States contributed to the paucity of literature concerning Latin America. The limited material published by Soviet scholars during the 1920's and 1930's was narrow in its approach, disorganized in its treatment, and unsatisfactory in its quality. The one "substantial" analysis of the Monroe Doctrine was that in the *Large Soviet Encyclopedia,* which subscribed to a simple but traditional interpretation, tinged with Marxist-Leninist views of history, that the Monroe Doctrine emerged as a reply to a Tsarist attempt to organize, with the aid of the Holy Alliance, a reactionary intervention in the affairs of the Latin-American republics. This antireactionary nature of the Monroe Doctrine, the Soviets argued, continued to exist until the 1860's when it was used against Napoleon III's adventure in Mexico. With the entry of the United States upon "an imperialist stage of development," the Soviets alleged that the United States government abandoned the original concept of the Monroe Doctrine—that of preventing foreign intrusion into the affairs of the Western Hemisphere—and turned it into a tool of its policy to intervene in Latin America, to enter the war with Spain, and during the Harding, Coolidge, and Hoover administrations to reserve "America for North Americans."

At the end of World War II, the Soviets modified their view. One of the main forces behind the modified view was the rise of revolutionary restlessness among the peoples of underdeveloped areas, including Latin America, which had occupied an important place in Soviet ideological pronouncements and long-range political strategy. The concentrated efforts to penetrate these regions ideologically, economically, and politically began after Stalin's death. The long-range aim of this penetration, which has varied in tactics from country to country, has been manifold. It has sought to exploit dissatisfaction in the less developed countries of the world with their present political and economic conditions. It has tried to foster the belief among the leaders of the underdeveloped countries that their poverty and present weakness stem from previous political status. It has hoped to establish a measure of good will, especially among politically articulate groups, by supporting their political, social, and economic objectives. It has attempted to portray all Western programs for these countries as merely a disguise for old "imperialism" intended to maintain the non-industrial countries in a state of economic subjugation. It has sought to present the U.S.S.R. as a benevolently disinterested "brother" and champion of underdeveloped countries in their struggle for economic independence. It has endeavored to identify itself with the national aspirations of new states and to create the impression that only the U.S.S.R. is interested in their industrialization. Finally, it has attempted to emphasize the superiority of the Soviet type of economy for rapid industrial development.

The enhanced Soviet interest in underdeveloped regions of the world, including Latin America, during the past decade has evolved into a major undertaking. This is evident by the growth of periodical literature and monographic studies, academic meetings, the organization during the summer of 1960 of the Soviet Association of Friendship and Cultural Cooperation with Latin American Countries, and the founding early in 1962 of a special Institute of Latin American Affairs at the Academy of Sciences of the U.S.S.R. The aim of the Institute is to publish works on Latin-American history, politics, economics, and culture, to coordinate Latin-American studies and research within the U.S.S.R. as well as in the countries of the Soviet bloc, to establish and to maintain contacts with Latin-American countries, and to train Soviet personnel qualified in Latin-American affairs. The Institute plans to publish a two-volume abstract on Latin America, a volume of articles on the recent national liberation and working-class movements, a symposium on contemporary problems of Brazil, and a volume dealing with "the success of socialist construction" in Cuba.

It was inevitable that this concentrated Soviet concern with Latin-American history and politics should lead to a reexamination of the nature of the Monroe Doctrine. The earliest indication of this change came in an article written for the *Large Soviet Encyclopedia* in 1954. According to the new version, the Monroe Doctrine emerged from the pressure of three forces: an intensified struggle between Britain and the United States for domination of Latin America, then in the process of emancipation from Portuguese and

Spanish colonial rule; a threat from the Holy Alliance, which sought to "suppress liberation movements" in Latin America; and expansionist tendencies of the United States. The Soviets contend that the last point was of decisive influence, and that the Monroe Doctrine in reality meant "America for the United States."

In addition to these contentions, the Soviets boldly asserted that from its inception the Monroe Doctrine has been employed by the United States government to camouflage its expansionist plans, and that this government, using the role of "protector" of the Western Hemisphere, has sought to subjugate the countries of Hispanic America by interfering in their affairs, by imposing on them "slave-like treaties," and by acquiring their territories. In the new Soviet view, the clearest expression of the aggressive nature of the Monroe Doctrine in its early stages of development was the Mexican War of 1846–48, which, it is claimed, netted the United States half the territory of Mexico. By the end of the nineteenth century, the "reactionary and aggressive nature" of the Monroe Doctrine became more pronounced and manifested itself in such designs as an "imperialist war" against Spain in 1898 (by which the United States acquired almost all of the Spanish colonies in the Pacific and the Caribbean); systematic interference by the United States in the affairs of Cuba, Mexico, Haiti, Nicaragua, Panama, Colombia, the Dominican Republic, and other countries of the Western Hemisphere; determined efforts to eliminate from the Western Hemisphere other capitalist competitors (especially Britain); and plans to organize a police force to protect the interests of the United States in Latin America. Building on this evidence of the United States's aggressiveness under the shield of the Monroe Doctrine, the Soviets allege that in the twentieth century the United States has expanded beyond the perimeter of the Western Hemisphere, has attempted to impose its will on China and other countries of Asia, has interfered in the affairs of European countries and by these actions has transformed the Monroe Doctrine into a weapon of its policy to establish domination over the rest of the world.

The new Soviet interpretation of the Monroe Doctrine received further elaboration by Nikolai N. Bolkhovitinov, a historian specializing in Latin America, in his book on *The*

Monroe Doctrine: Its Origin and Nature. Published by the Institute of International Relations in Moscow and based on a rather extensive examination of non-Russian and Russian literature (both published and unpublished), this 335-page monograph represents the first major and detailed Soviet study of the Monroe Doctrine. Its importance lies mainly in its unqualified rejection of the standard and known scholarly interpretations of the Doctrine, and above all in its persistent emphasis that the famous declaration was a product of two principal forces: aggressive capitalism, which, it is argued, always and everywhere "is inseparably bound up with violence, with wars, with aggression and the subjugation of weak nations," and militant bourgeois nationalism, which seeks to increase its "sphere of influence."

To support the thesis that "aggressive capitalism" was a major instigator of the Monroe Doctrine, Bolkhovitinov has advanced an interesting argument. He opposes the view that the United States was an agrarian nation until the second half of the nineteenth century and insists that as early as the end of the War of 1812 the United States (and especially New England) was a rapidly developing capitalist country. In defense of this contention he cites the growth and mechanization of the textile industry; the rise of numerous industrial and commercial families; a substantial increase of capital; the great upsurge of metallurgy; the growth of the merchant marine with a corresponding expansion of commercial relations with the rest of the world; increased employment of people in industry and resulting urbanization; the building of roads, canals, and harbors; the enactment of the Tariff of 1816 "aimed at creating a domestic market"; and the development of economic bonds between northern capitalists and southern plantation owners. Bolkhovitinov maintains that these and other "indicators of maturing aggressive capitalism" gave an impetus to expansionist tendencies and the quest for new markets.

According to Bolkhovitinov, the expansion of this "aggressive capitalism" assumed two basic directions: northern and southern. The principal leaders of the former were representatives of the bourgeoisie, land speculators, rich fur traders, mining companies, lumbermen, farmers, European emigrants and workers. The chief spokesmen of southern expansion were slave-owning planters who had come under

the "patriarchal protection" of northern and British capitalists. In his opinion, the southern expansion was more aggressive and accordingly played a more decisive role in the
development of the Monroe Doctrine. To "prove" this thesis
he cites the increase in cotton exports between 1816 and
1827 and suggests that this increase (in view of the slaves'
lack of interest in increased production and the absence of
advanced technology) could have come only with territorial
expansion.

Bolkhovitinov acknowledges that incorporation of new
territories into the expanding capitalist system has helped
the development of the productive forces of the area. He
stresses, however, that this expansion was not idyllic, as
American historians would like one to believe, but on the
contrary was accomplished through brutal treatment of the
Indians and ruthless encroachments on possessions of Britain, France, Spain, Russia, and Mexico. Bolkhovitinov is
also critical of the failure of American historians to see the
connection between territorial expansion and the desire to
extend the slave economy. His criticism is based on the
theory that United States historians explain this expansion
by giving credit to favorable national factors and poor farmers and not to the slave owners who actually spearheaded
the westward movement in the south.

The second force which, in Bolkhovitinov's view, exercised profound influence on the Monroe Doctrine was
"militant bourgeois nationalism." While he acknowledges
the progressive contributions of the United States in such
declarations as peoples' sovereignty and the inalienable
right of the people to rebel, he argues, nevertheless, that by
its very nature as a bourgeois state the United States was
propelled toward nationalism and expansion of its sphere of
influence. He contends that expansionist tendencies already
present in the colonial period assumed the form of "messian-
ism" and "providential exclusiveness" in the early national
period and culminated in the Monroe Doctrine of 1823. To
support this thesis, he cites such evidence as the Louisiana
Purchase of 1803; the acquisition of Florida in 1819; the
penetration into Texas in the early 1820's; an interest in
Cuba; and selected passages from the writings of Jefferson,
Franklin, G. Morris, Clay, Calhoun, Jackson, Benton, and
John Q. Adams—individuals who, he states, subscribed to
the concepts of "natural frontiers," "geographic symmetry,"

"control of river mouths," "exits to the sea," "Manifest Destiny," and the "American system."

Having convinced himself that the Monroe Doctrine was a product of two selfish and aggressive forces—capitalism and nationalism—Bolkhovitinov then questions the validity of certain standard interpretations of the Monroe Doctrine. He repudiates, for instance, the idea that the Monroe Doctrine was intended to benefit Latin-American people and cites as evidence an anti-Latin-American attitude on the part of leaders in the United States; a consideration of Latin America by various United States officials as an appendage of the United States; a racial bias and belief by southern plantation owners that Hispanic-American peoples were subhuman; a feeling among the people of the United States that they had nothing in common with their southern neighbors; the supplying of arms to royalists in Latin America by the United States; and an unwillingness on the part of the United States government to support revolutionary movements in the Western Hemisphere. The cardinal weakness of his "evidence" lies in Bolkhovitinov's apparent gross ignorance of political processes in the United States and above all in his naive assumption (or his deliberate misrepresentation) that a speech from the floor of Congress by any legislator on an opinion voiced by any important individual invariably represents a policy of the United States government. This assumption has led him throughout his study to innumerable rash generalizations that cannot be substantiated.

Bolkhovitinov is also highly critical of the interpretation that the Monroe Doctrine was primarily defensive in nature—a response, as it were, to threats from the Holy Alliance in Latin America and from Russia in the Pacific Northwest. He categorically states that there was no real threat to Latin America and that no real plans of intervention were considered by the members of the Holy Alliance. He further maintains that the prospect of a reestablishment of Spanish domination in America was absurd, that the United States government was aware of the nonexistence of such "threats," and that these threats were manufactured by the British and United States governments and press to enable them, while posing as protectors of the Western Hemisphere, "to gain political advantage." Needless to say,

Bolkhovitinov's failure to "discover" the presence of a European threat to the Western Hemisphere reinforces his preconceived thesis that the Monroe Doctrine was motivated by selfish interests of the United States and not by the interests of Spanish colonies struggling for their independence; that it was an expression of the aggressive policy inherent in every "bourgeois state"; and that from the Western Hemisphere this "aggressive tendency" of the United States spread subsequently throughout the entire world—a reasoning which, as we noted, was first expressed in the 1954 edition of the Soviet encyclopedia.

Soviet views on the origin, purpose, and development of the Monroe Doctrine, which have been summarized briefly in the preceding pages, and especially those expounded since 1954, raise two basic questions: What is the aim of this unusual presentation of distorted evidence? And for what audience or purpose is this evidence intended? To answer these questions is not an easy task, because our knowledge of the exact Soviet intentions in Latin America is inadequate. The following, however, is certain. Since 1954, Soviet interest in Hispanic America has rapidly and systematically increased and has led to numerous cultural exchanges, visits, trade exhibitions, trade agreements and above all to persistent assertions, both official and unofficial, that the U.S.S.R. is a selfless friend of Latin-American peoples while the United States is their chief oppressor and exploiter, past and present. With Cuba, Soviet relations since 1959 have developed into a close cultural, political, economic, and military tie—a development which has presented the spirit of the Monroe Doctrine, and indeed the entire Western Hemisphere, with its most formidable challenge to date. Intoxicated by their apparent success and convinced that "the Monroe Doctrine was dead," the Soviets ignored all warnings about their encroachments in the Western Hemisphere. Late in 1962, Soviet overconfidence led to a direct military confrontation, which resulted in a partial Soviet withdrawal of offensive weapons from Cuba. The resolute action of the United States and the cooperative support of many OAS members during and following the height of the Cuban crisis of 1962 indicated that the spirit of the Monroe Doctrine—that of keeping foreign influence **out** of the Western Hemisphere—was far from dead.

Note on Sources

The effects of the Monroe Doctrine on the publishing industry have been almost as explosive as its effects on international relations and politics. It has produced a plethora of books, articles, editorials, pamphlets, and published speeches.

Standard studies of the Monroe Doctrine and of its relation to Pan-Americanism are, for the United States, four volumes by Dexter Perkins, as follows: *The Monroe Doctrine, 1823–1826*, Cambridge, Mass., 1927; *The Monroe Doctrine, 1826–1867*, Baltimore, 1933; *The Monroe Doctrine, 1867–1907*, Baltimore, 1937; and *A History of the Monroe Doctrine*, Boston, 1955. The background of the Doctrine, emphasizing John Quincy Adams's role in formulating it, is given in Samuel Flagg Bemis, *John Quincy Adams and the Foundations of American Foreign Policy*, New York, 1949, chaps. 18 and 19. The contributions of Jefferson are shown in Theodore R. Schellenberg, "Jeffersonian Origins of the Monroe Doctrine," *Hispanic American Historical Review*, XIV, 1–32, February 1934.

The British background of the Monroe Doctrine is presented in two books by Charles K. Webster, *The Foreign Policy of Castlereagh, 1815–1822: Britain and the European Alliance*, London, 1958, and *Britain and the Independence of Latin America, 1812–1830*, 2 vols., London and New York, 1938; and by H. W. V. Temperley in his *Foreign Policy of Canning, 1822–27*, London, 1925.

Latin-American inspiration for the Monroe Doctrine is stressed in Alejandro Álvarez, *The Monroe Doctrine: Its Importance in the International Life of the States of the New World*, New York, 1924, and Diego de la Peña, *La Doctrina de Monroe*, Bogotá, 1949. On the other hand the ideas of Monroe and his associates are contrasted with those of Bolívar favoring Latin-American unity and fraternity in Gaston Nerval (Raúl Díez de Medina), *Autopsy of the Monroe Doctrine: The Strange Story of Inter-American Relations*, New York, 1934; José Vasconcelos, *Bolivarismo y Monroísmo*, Santiago de Chile, 1937; and Ezéquiel Ramírez Novoa, *Monroísmo y Bolivarismo en América Latina*, Buenos Aires, 1957.

Notable histories of the origins of the Monroe Doctrine, its application and its implications for inter-American relations, are

Herbert Kraus *Die Monroedoktrin in ihren Beziehungen zur Amerikanischen Diplomatie und zum Völkerrecht*, Berlin, 1913; and Camilo Barcía Trelles, *Le Doctrine de Monroë dans son développement historique, particulièrement en ce qui concerne les relations Interaméricaines*, Paris, 1931. Relevant diplomatic documents on the history of the Doctrine are published in John Bassett Moore, *Digest of International Law*, Washington, 1906, vol. VI, and Green Haywood Hackworth, *Digest of International Law*, Washington 1940– , vol. V.

The relation of Canada to the Monroe Doctrine is traced in Pierre Sebilleau, *Le Canada et la Doctrine de Monroe*, Paris, 1937; and a Canadian interpretation of Monroeism and Pan-Americanism is presented in John P. Humphrey, *The Inter-American System: A Canadian View*, Toronto, 1942. Brazil's relation to the Monroe Doctrine and Pan-Americanism is discussed in Helio Lobo, *O Pan-americanismo e o Brasil*, São Paulo, 1939. Studies in a broader Latin-American perspective include Enrique Gil, *Evolución del Pan-americanismo*, Buenos Aires, 1933, and Jesús M. Yepes, *La Philosophie du panaméricanisme*, Neuchâtel, 1945. Argentina's relation to the Doctrine is shown in Raúl Rodríguez Araya, "La Doctrina Monroe y la República Argentina," *Revista de Derecho Internacional*, Havana, vol. 59, pp. 454–471, December 31, 1951. In José María Rosa, "La Doctrina de Monroe y su Aplicación en la República Argentina," *Revista de Ciencias Jurídicas y Sociales*, Universidad Nacional del Litoral, Santa Fe, Argentina, tercera época, año 9, no. 41, 1944, pp. 5–29, an Argentine professor of international law advances the thesis that Argentina, rather than the United States, has been the chief upholder of the real Monroe Doctrine.

Soviet Russia and other Communist countries have given much attention to the Monroe Doctrine, as follows: Ignacy Sachs, "Polityka Stanów Zjednoczonych Wobec Krajów Ameryki Yacinskiej," *Kwartalnik Historyczny*, 1955, 283–293; M. Antiasov and A. Glinken, "Novoe v Panamerikanisme," *Mezhdunarodnaya Zhizn*, no. 12, December 1957, pp. 93–105; and S. Gonionskiy, "Nepogrebenniy trup 'Doktriny Monro,'" *Mezhdunarodnaya Zhizn*, 1960, no. 10, pp. 82–90, published in English as "The Unburied Corpse of the Monroe Doctrine," *International Affairs*, Moscow, October 1960, pp. [60]–66. A Soviet study dealing with the origins of the Doctrine and the immediate reactions to it is Nikolai N. Bolkhovitinov, *Doktrina Monro: Proiskhozhdenie i Kharakter*, Moscow, 1959.

The Monroe Doctrine in the Venezuelan crisis of 1895 is reviewed in G. B. Young, "Intervention under the Monroe Doctrine: the Olney Corollary," *Political Science Quarterly*, vol. 57,

247–280, June 1942; and W. LaFeber, "Background of Cleveland's Venezuelan Policy: A Reinterpretation," *American Historical Review,* vol. 66, 947–967, July 1961. Theodore Roosevelt's interpretations of the Doctrine are discussed in J. Fred Rippy, "Antecedents of the Roosevelt Corollary of the Monroe Doctrine," *Pacific Historical Review,* IX, 267–279, September 1940. The genesis of the Roosevelt Corollary and subsequent applications of it are reviewed in Dana G. Munro, *Intervention and Dollar Diplomacy in the Caribbean, 1900–1921,* Princeton, 1964. The Lodge Corollary is analyzed in Thomas A. Bailey, "Lodge Corollary to the Monroe Doctrine," *Political Science Quarterly,* vol. 48, 220–239, June 1933. The history of the no-transfer principle is traced in John A. Logan, *No Transfer, an American Security Principle,* New Haven, 1961, and the non-intervention principle is the subject of Alberto Arroyo Rivera, *La No Intervención en el Derecho Internacional Americano,* Mexico, 1952, comparing the doctrines of Monroe, Calvo, Drago, and Estrada in this respect.

Pursuing the suggestion of Uruguay's President Baltasar Brum, Arístides L. Delle Piane, *Doctrina de Monroe,* Montevideo, 1930, concludes that any threat to the independence of any of the American states, whether it comes from outside or from inside the Americas, is contrary to the Monroe Doctrine. The subsequent multilateralization or Pan-Americanization of the Doctrine is the theme of William R. Castle, "Monroe Doctrine and Pan Americanism," *Annals of the American Academy,* vol. 204, pp. 111–118, July 1939; Philip C. Jessup, "The Monroe Doctrine in 1940," *American Journal of International Law,* October 1940, pp. 704–711; Dexter Perkins, "Bringing the Monroe Doctrine up to Date," *Foreign Affairs,* vol. 20, [253]–265, January 1942; Richard K. Showman and Lyman S. Judson, comps., "The Monroe Doctrine and the Growth of Western Hemisphere Solidarity," *Reference Shelf,* vol. 14, no. 7, New York, 1941; Eduardo Albanell Mac Coll, "Continentalización de la Doctrina de Monroe," *Boletín del Ministerio de Relaciones Exteriores,* Uruguay, April 1943, pp. 9–13; and Teodoro Alvarado Garaicoa, *El Imperialismo y la Democracia a Través de la Doctrina Monroe,* Guayaquil, 1946. Latin-American reactions to the Monroe Doctrine and the various steps in the Pan-Americanization of the Doctrine after 1930 are presented in Donald Marquand Dozer, *Are We Good Neighbors? Three Decades of Inter-American Relations, 1930–1960,* Gainesville, Florida, 1959, *passim.*

A bibliography of published materials on the Monroe Doctrine after 1929 will be found in Pan American Union, *Index to*

Latin American Periodical Literature, 1929–1960, vol. 5, Boston, Massachusetts, 1962. In 1941 the United States Senate included a "Selected Bibliography on the Monroe Doctrine, with Special Reference to its Modern Aspects," in its publication *Senate Document no. 303,* 76th Congress, 3d Session. Other essential bibliographical aids to recent writings on the subject include the *Handbook of Latin American Studies,* 1936–   , Cambridge and Gainesville; *Reader's Guide to Periodical Literature,* 1900–   , New York; and *Public Affairs Information Service,* 1915–   , New York.

A NOTE ON THE TYPE

The text of this book is set in Caledonia, a typeface designed by W(illiam) A(ddison) Dwiggins for the Mergenthaler Linotype Company in 1939. Dwiggins chose to call his new typeface Caledonia, the Roman name for Scotland, because it was inspired by the Scotch types cast about 1833 by Alexander Wilson & Son, Glasgow type founders. However, there is a calligraphic quality about this face that is totally lacking in the Wilson types. Dwiggins referred to an even earlier typeface for this "liveliness of action"—one cut around 1790 by William Martin for the printer William Bulmer. Caledonia has more weight than the Martin letters, and the bottom finishing strokes (serifs) of the letters are cut straight across, without brackets, to make sharp angles with the upright stems, thus giving a "modern face" appearance.

W. A. Dwiggins (1880–1956) was born in Martinsville, Ohio, and studied art in Chicago. In 1904 he moved to Hingham, Massachusetts, where he built a solid reputation as a designer of advertisements and as a calligrapher. He began an association with the Mergenthaler Linotype Company in 1929, and over the next twenty-seven years designed a number of book types for that firm. Of especial interest are the Metro series, Electra, Caledonia, Eldorado, and Falcon. In 1930, Dwiggins first became interested in marionettes, and through the years made many important contributions to the art of puppetry and the design of marionettes.